ALLITEI

INSPIRATION:

GALATIANS

Finding True Freedom

FIRST BOOK IN THE SERIES
THE BOOK OF GALATIANS

Graham Albert Logan

MMedSc, BSc Hons, Dip Th, Dip Pastoral

This book is dedicated to my late father, Thomas John Logan, who loved many books but lived in the Book of Books and therein had found true freedom and lived it quietly and unassumingly. He never had the opportunity to publish any books but if he had his books would have been awesome. It is because of his godly influence that this book has been humbly written in his memory.

Also to the memory of the Reverend David Hamill who went home to be with the Lord on Sunday 24th January 2021. David is fondly remembered as the highly esteemed Pastor of First Church of the Nazarene, Skegoneill Avenue, Belfast, a great friend, a loving mentor and a close brother in Christ.

David was instrumental in bringing many to experience the redeeming and restoring power of Christ and the true freedom that was purchased by Divine blood on the hill of Golgotha, including the author.

When the eternal day dawns and the shadows flee away, many will testify on that great day to the ministry and witness of the Rev. David who exemplified a life lived in the joy of the fullness of freedom in our Lord Jesus Christ, to whom be all the glory both now and for evermore,
Amen.

CONTENTS

ACKNOWLEDGEMENTS

I would like to acknowledge my publishing team for all their help and support in getting this book to publication; without them it would have been quite impossible. Their advice and expertise is second to none.

I would like to acknowledge my dog Barney, my wonderful Harrier Hound who was with me for every single hour over the many months of thinking, meditating and writing. The long walks for further thinking were a welcome interlude from the writing desk that my dad used for many years of study.

FOREWORD

The Bible is the Word of God. We need to read it and hear what God is saying to us today. It needs to have the proper place and priority in our lives. The series 'Alliteration for Inspiration' has been written as a facilitating tool to aid our exploration of the Holy Scriptures.

About Alliteration For Inspiration

Its Purpose
The purpose is to act as a **stimulus** to stimulate in us the desire to read the Word of God. Let us learn to read the Word slowly and carefully and not be in a rush.

Its Plan
The plan is to provide us with a **structure** and **summary** in the form of alliteration to get us to think about what is written in the Book of books.

Its Pointers

The pointers i.e. the alliteration are presented so as to act as a humble **servant** to get us to immerse ourselves in Scriptures and aid our grasp of what is written, for herein is the secret of the freedom we have been longing for.

Its Priority

The priority in focus is that we might not only **study** the Book of books but that we get to know the Author of the book, The God of the Book.

Its Place

It goes without saying that alliteration for inspiration is but **secondary**! It ambitiously seeks to provide a systematic and synthesising tool, i.e. the tool of alliteration, to get us into the Word.

Never before was there such an urgency that we give time and space and place to the Word of God.

So many voices are clamouring to be heard. We need to hear the Word of God. We need to listen to the God of the Word. God speaks through His Word today.

Its Prerogative

It seeks to use alliteration as a set of **signposts**

ultimately pointing to the blessed one who said:

> You search the Scriptures because you think
> that in them you have eternal life; and it is they
> that bear witness about me.
> John 5.39 {ESV}

> Then He opened their minds so they could
> understand the Scriptures.
> Luke 24.45 {ESV}

As we get into the Word Of God, may the Lord open our minds also so that we too might understand the Scriptures of Truth and deepen our relationship with the One who is the Way, The Truth and the Life. The One who bought our freedom on the Hill called Calvary.

Its Plea

Let us see to it that we **search** the Scriptures for ourselves as the Beareans did in the Acts of the Apostles; rather the 'Acts' of the Holy Spirit.

> Now these (Bearean) Jews were more noble than
> those in Thessalonica; they received the word
> with all eagerness, examining the Scriptures daily

to see if these things were so.

Acts 17.11 {ESV}

Its Potential

This book has the potential to act as a **scout** or a **guide** to get us to really, really read the Word carefully with diligence and effectiveness.

It is my earnest prayer that the Holy Spirit Himself will use this tool to act as a **springboard** so that we enthusiastically delve into the Scriptures of Truth and understand and adhere to what is written therein.

> The Ethiopian Treasurer, a court official of Candace, Queen of the Ethiopians was returning on his journey from Jerusalem and on the road to Gaza he was reading the Word. At the direction of the Holy Spirit, Philip was instructed to join him.
>
> So Philip ran to him and heard him reading Isaiah the prophet and asked, "Do you understand what you are reading?"
>
> And he said, "How can I, unless someone guides me?" And he invited Philip to come up and sit with him.
>
> Acts 8.30,31 {ESV}

Let us read the Word on our journey through life and may this book on Galatians be a good companion to help us in our reading of the Holy Scriptures and humbly fulfil the objectives for which it was indeed written as set out heretofore.

I pray that God will use this book to encourage you to get into the Bible for yourself. That the Lord Jesus Christ will be glorified through it. That believers will be drawn closer to our Lord and Master and that those who are not yet in Christ will be brought to faith in Him alone for salvation.

Sincerely yours in Christ,

Graham Albert Logan

February, 2021

Banbridge, Co. Down, Northern Ireland

INTRODUCTION

Inspiration of Scripture

> All Scripture is breathed out by God and profitable for teaching, for reproof, for correction, and for training in righteousness, that the man of God may be complete, equipped for every good work.
> 2 Timothy 3:16-17 {ESV}

All Scripture is inspired by God. The Bible is God's chosen means of communication to all of humanity in this present dispensation. This is how God communicates with us today. If we want to know what God is saying to us then we really need to read His Word and meditate on His Word. If we don't read the Word how do we expect to know what God is saying to us?

Don't just take my word for it. Read it for yourself. Make this a regular and daily habit. Meditate upon the Word. Think about it. Ask God to speak to you through it.

Get a reading plan and set aside time each day to be alone with God and His Word. Find ways and means for getting into the Scriptures, really into the depths of the Word – get to grips with the passages and seek the help of the Holy Spirit. He is our Divine Teacher.

There is nothing to be compared to being in the presence of the Living God and in His Living Word.

The Bible is still the best-selling book in the world. It deserves your attention and time.

Word saturation

Allowing His Word to live in us! He has promised to lead and guide us.

> Your word is a lamp to my feet and a light to my path.
> Psalm 119:105 {ESV}

His Word will keep us from sin.

His book will keep us from sin. Or sin will keep us from this book.

> I have stored up your word in my heart that I might not sin against you.
> Psalm 119:11 {ESV}

Just to reiterate, this book employs a particular means or method for getting into the Word of God, it's called alliteration.

Definition of alliteration

The occurrence of the same letter or sound at the beginning of adjacent or closely connected words.

The Wikipedia definition:
In the Wikipedia definition, alliteration is the conspicuous repetition of identical initial consonant sounds in successive or closely associated syllables within a group of words, even those spelled differently. As a method of linking words for effect, alliteration is also called head rhyme or initial rhyme.

The reason for using alliteration is that it sounds pleasing to the ear and it's a means to get the attention of readers or listeners. It's also a clear way to signify that the alliterative words are linked together thematically and puts a spotlight on the subject matter contained therein.

My personal experience is that it really helps me get into the Word. I am sharing this with you in the belief that it could prove advantageous to you as well. Passages can be set out in a way that helps us to think of the content but also can act as a mnemonic.

Alliteration can be a great help to annotators and experienced students of the Word as well as for those who are new to the Word and for whom chapters and long sections of scripture can seem difficult to get a handle on. Alliteration can also be useful for pastors and teachers and preachers and used as good solid pegs to hang material on.

This can also work in the favour of congregations who can take the points away with them as well as helping them concentrate on what is being presented. Have you ever asked someone, 'What was the speaker speaking about?' And have you ever discovered that a number of people have a problem telling you what the message was? Alliteration is a tried and tested method for helping us to remember.

Try it and see. Alliteration for inspiration. It's a technique worth having and using. The important thing is that you are getting into the Word of God every day. The Bible is the Book of Books. Whatever else you are reading, make sure that the Bible is the number one Book in your life.

C H Spurgeon put it most aptly and succinctly by saying: *"Visit many good books but live in the Bible."*

The purpose of this book is to help you utilise the tool of alliteration and get into the Word of God for yourself.

It's important to point out that like anything else alliteration can be taken to extremes so we need to be careful in our use of alliteration.

We don't want the alliteration to become burdensome and even nonsensical.

Many years ago when I was a student at theological college, a fellow student was preparing a message and decided to use words ending in 'ation' (e.g. Salvation, Adoption and so forth) to pin his material on and get the message across.

He asked his peers if they could help with the final 'ation' for his message. Someone said flippantly, 'What about Bus-station?' We all laughed heartily. The point being, you can go too far with alliteration and end up lost in 'transit', if you pardon the pun!

One more thing. There are quite a lot of headings given in this book – the idea is to take what is useful to you and make the most of them – but the priority is to get into the Word. Have a look at the headings and use them to get you to think about what is written in Galatians.

One other point I would like to make at this juncture is that I have deliberately included Bible verses in the text. The priority is the Word of God, therefore the book sets out the chapter verses in the text and then where appropriate other verses from other parts of the Bible have been carefully selected and included that help to elucidate the Bible verses being considered. The reason for this is that the best commentary on the Bible is the Bible. The profound complementarity of the Bible is astounding and is just one of the many evidences of its authenticity – it is the Living Word of the Living God.

I find that alliteration helps me to read the passage slowly and carefully. We can read much too fast and miss so much. We need to slow down and allow the words to permeate our hearts and souls and minds. As you read, ideas form and inform our thinking which will impact on our outlook and our attitudes and our behaviour.

> The Holy Spirit who is the Spirit of Truth is the One who leads us into all truth. Jesus said;
> And you shall know the truth, and the truth shall make you free.
> John 8.32. {NKJV}

For me I find that the Holy Spirit brings words to my mind that help me to get the content of the passage in mind and this is where I find that alliteration works.

Perhaps you can come up with other words and improve on what is written here. The words used here are not exhaustive but words that came to the author when meditating on the scriptures of truth in the Scriptures of Truth over the past year of Covid-19.

Enough said.

Let's get into Galatians!

CHAPTER 1

NO OTHER GOSPEL

Outline/Overview of chapter One

V1-5 Paul's Sovereign Appointment

V6-10 Paul's Serious Astonishment

V11-24 Paul's Sovereign Assignment

V1-5 Paul's Sovereign Appointment

V1. Paul, an apostle—not from men nor through man, but through Jesus Christ and God the Father, who raised him from the dead—

V2. and all the brothers who are with me,

V3. Grace to you and peace from God our Father and the Lord Jesus Christ,

V4. who gave Himself for our sins to deliver us from the present evil age, according to the will of our God and Father,

V5. to whom be the glory forever and ever. Amen.

In these opening verses Paul says some astounding things about his calling, his work and life's mission. It is all of God from beginning to the end.
Here we are introduced to the following in V1-5:

Paul's Divine Apostleship
Right at the beginning Paul states his apostolic authority.

Paul's Divine Appointment
Paul was appointed through Jesus Christ and God the father.

Paul's Divine Authority
His authority does not come from human commission or human authorities but from being Divinely appointed.
Almost 30% of the New Testament was written by Paul under the inspiration and authority of the Holy Spirit.

Paul's Divine Authentication
Paul was authentic and right at the start he states that this authenticity comes from the Lord. Are we

authentic? Authentic Christians. Do we have Divine authentication?

Paul was not only a man who had been appointed by God to be an Apostle, he was under that same authority and his authenticity comes from God.

Today there are many who would claim to have the same status as Paul and demand to be heard on the basis of Divine authority and Divine authenticity! But whoever claims this Divine authority must also live under that Divine authority.

And how do we know that a person is living under Divine authority? They are living by the Word of God, and what they teach adheres to the Word of God.

That is why we need to read the Bible for ourselves. God's will never goes contrary to His Word.

When people say this is the Gospel then take note. Is it in keeping with God's Word?

That was the inherent problem that existed in the churches of Galatia. Several Christian communities had come under the influence of false teachers who also claimed Divine authority and Divine authenticity for their teaching. But their teaching and way of life did not match the authoritative Word of God.

Watch out when people come and declare you

should do this! You should do that! This is what God wants you to do!

If it is contrary to the Word of God then ignore them. The Bible is the final authority, not the word of a self-proclaimed prophet claiming Divine authority.

You just have to read through books like the Book of Jeremiah to find that many of the Pastors and Shepherds of the People of Israel were not what they said they were and their words were not the Words of God.

They were people pleasers, like the false teachers in Galatia who liked to tickle the ears of their audiences and entrap them into their own facade of what we could call 'whited sepulchrism'. This was the term that Jesus referred to when speaking of the religious leaders at that time. Looking all nice on the outside but full of dead bones on the inside.

I am not seeking to undermine those pastors who are God-fearing wise Shepherds; indeed they would welcome this highlighting of the difference and distinction between those who claim to have Divine authority and use it to usurp their own agenda, ideas and programmes and those who seek to proclaim the whole counsel of God from a humble heart that is subservient to Christ and who truly have the Divine authority in their authentic calling to speak for God.

Paul's Divine Associates

The Apostle Paul makes it clear that he is appointed by none other than God Himself and he is not alone for everyone who is truly in Christ has also been Divinely appointed and has the same Divine authority.

Paul's appointment was to the office of Apostleship. Wherein have we been appointed?

A reading of 1 Corinthians Chapter 12 elaborates on this train of thought. Verse 12 states that:

> God has placed and arranged the parts of the body, each one of them, just as He willed and saw fit with the best balance of function. {AMP}

Paul speaks of the body of Believers – the Church – the body of Christ and every one of us is to find our function in the body.

Paul's function was as an Apostle. What is yours? What is mine?

Find it because you have been Divinely appointed to it. Find your niche –

Find your calling in Christ and do it.

We too like Paul are Divine appointees.

'If God calls you to be a missionary don't stoop to be a king.'
{Missionary quote by Jordan Grooms}

Gladys May Aylward was an English missionary in China and Taiwan. Born on February 24, 1902, in Edmonton, North of London, England, she died of influenza on January 2, 1970, in Taipei, Taiwan. Gladys was the daughter of a postman and a postal worker and she left school at fourteen to work as a shop assistant and later she worked as a domestic. Gladys became a Christian believer at age eighteen in 1920.

As a young woman she read a newspaper commentary about China and the millions of people who had never heard of the Gospel. This article was to change her life.

She sought training at the China Inland Mission (C.I.M.) in London, but she soon found the study of theology and languages difficult and after three months in the program, the chair of the C.I.M. committee reported:

"It is with great regret that I have to recommend to you that we do not accept Miss Aylward. She has a call to serve God—she is sincere and courageous—but we cannot take the responsibility of sending a woman of 26, with such limited Christian experience and education, to China."

She was also too old, he felt, to learn the Chinese language.

But she was appointed by God and whom God calls He equips. She went on to be a mighty missionary for God and was called the virtuous one by the Chinese people.

Gladys was appointed by the same authority as Paul and she lived her life under that same authority, and her Divine role in life was possible even when others thought it impossible and even tried to stop her for being, in their estimation, inadequate, unsuitable and just not up to the task.

Paul was rejected too; in his case it was by the Rabbinic schools of his day but he was chosen by God and that is all that mattered.

His was:

A Divine Mandate

Find your function because you too are under Divine mandate! We are mandated to serve God. That is our primary mandate! Find your ministry because you are mandated to do it.

Do not for one second think that you are insignificant or unimportant or even irrelevant; that is the enemy's lie to keep you from doing what you were put on this earth to do.

Paul was in reality an insignificant entity as a pharicial pharisee! But God had a mighty task for him to do and that made him significant. It was the God-given task that made him significant. And he never forgot it. Nearing the end of his letter to the churches in Galatia, Paul records these words:

> But far be it from me to boast except in the cross of our Lord Jesus Christ, by which the world has been crucified to me, and I to the world.
> Galatians, Chapter 6, Verse 14 {ESV}

You are not mandated to write a third of the New Testament. Paul was.

But the task that God has mandated for you to do is significant in the eyes of God. You are significant and the task God has for you is significant because your significance is found in God!

Jesus says to the disciples:

> You did not choose me, but I chose you and appointed you that you should go and bear fruit and that your fruit should abide, so that whatever you ask the Father in my name, he may give it to you.
>
> John, Chapter 15, V16. {ESV}

I don't know what your specific ministry is, but I do know this; if you ask Him He will tell you what it is because as surely as He chose those first disciples, He has assuredly chosen you and His will for you is to go and fulfil the ministry you were appointed to so that you should bear fruit that will remain for eternity.

We have wasted enough time on things that don't matter compared to fulfilling God's purpose for us.

We need balance, of course. You may have heard the phrase: 'He/she is so heavenly minded that they are no earthly use.'

We can smile at that but it can be sadly true.

Of course God does not want you to neglect your responsibilities as a father or a mother or a son or a daughter. Of course God does not want you to deny your responsibilities as a husband or a wife. Of course God expects the best of you as an employer or an employee or a volunteer.

All these things matter and there is plenty in Scripture to tell us how effectively these roles can be fulfilled. But this does not negate the fact that God has a ministry for you right where you are and right now. And He has a plan for your future – find it and do it!

And in finding it God will make sure it has a positive impact on every part of your life – everything will be influenced by this ministry.

A Divine Ministry

You have a ministry that only you can do! Find it and fulfil it!

Ministry? We can have a narrow view of 'Ministry'. We tend to think of Ministers who are trained in a theological college and then they are called to minister in a church as ministers who minister the Word and all this is true and we need God-fearing people to be called into the ministry.

But there is more to this than we might think. Perhaps a story by way of illustration might help.

A well-known evangelist/Minister was invited to a church to conduct a gospel mission. He arranged with the church to have an opening service which he called 'meet the team night'.

Everyone was pretty excited at the prospect of this great man of God coming to their church and they could not wait to meet his team.

The evening duly arrived and so did the evangelist. He sat quietly and then the local Pastor called on him to introduce the team. Some people thought, *Oh, the team must be waiting in the wings and he is going to call them out one by one.*

He began his remarks. "I have been so looking forward to being with you for this time of mission and outreach and I have been so looking forward to meeting the team – YOU are the team! YOU are the team."

We are all part of the team and we all have a ministry. Check out for further study what the Bible really says about ministry. For our purpose one passage of scripture will suffice.

V7. But grace was given to each one of us according to the measure of Christ's gift.

V8. Therefore it says,
"When he ascended on high he led a host of captives, and he gave gifts to men."

V9. (In saying, "He ascended," what does it mean but that he had also descended into the lower regions, the earth?

V10. He who descended is the one who also ascended far above all the heavens, that he might fill all things.)

V11. And he gave the apostles, the prophets, the evangelists, the shepherds and teachers,

V12. to equip the saints for the work of ministry, for building up the body of Christ,

V13. until we all attain to the unity of the faith and of the knowledge of the Son of God, to mature manhood, to the measure of the stature of the fullness of Christ,

V14. so that we may no longer be children, tossed to and fro by the waves and carried about by every wind of doctrine, by human cunning, by craftiness in deceitful schemes.

V15. Rather, speaking the truth in love, we are to grow up in every way into him who is the head, into Christ,

V16. from whom the whole body, joined and held together by every joint with which it is equipped, when each part is working properly, makes the body grow so that it builds itself up in love.

Ephesians, Chapter 4, Verses 7-16 {ESV}

Notice verse 12:

To equip the saints for the work of the ministry!

The AMP renders the verse in this way:

And He did this to fully equip and perfect the saints (God's people) for works of service.

The message Bible helps us with even more clarity.

V.7-13 But that doesn't mean you should all look and speak and act the same. Out of the generosity of Christ, each of us is given his own gift.
Notice that Paul refers to each being given their own gift.
And Jesus,

He climbed the high mountain,

He captured the enemy and seized the booty,

He handed it all out in gifts to the people.

Is it not true that the One who climbed up also climbed down, down to the valley of earth? And the One who climbed down is the One who climbed back up, up to highest heaven.

He handed out gifts above and below, filled heaven with his gifts, filled earth with his gifts. He handed out gifts of apostle, prophet, evangelist, and pastor-teacher – To train Christ's followers in skilled servant work, working within Christ's body, the church.

So every member in the entire church body is to be trained in skilled servant work. No, you don't necessarily need to go to a college to do that – the local church has leaders who have the responsibility to train every person. In fact, the MSG is a paraphrase and is therefore a way of expressing the meaning in a different range of words to clarify the meaning – which is good but is not always accurate.

The ESV uses the word 'equip'. The Greek word for equip is transliterated 'katartismos' and it means to prepare, to equip, to bring to a place of fitness. It comes from a word that means literally the complete furnishing of – hence the KJV rendering as the perfecting of. I think the best word is 'equip'. So we all have a ministry – and the evangelist who introduces the team was right – you are the team. We are the Team!

The MSG continues until we're all moving rhythmically and easily with each other, efficient and graceful in response to God's Son, fully mature adults, fully developed within and without, fully alive like Christ.

As yes – we need maturity – we need to be fully developed.

My friend at theological college many years ago was asked by an academic, "And what was your education?"

"At St. Mary's, sir," was the reply.

"And which St. Mary's was that?"

"Down at the feet of Jesus, sir," was the reply.

There is no substitute and no better place for being equipped and matured than sitting at Jesus's feet as Mary did.

It was said of the disciples Peter and John that the people took knowledge of them because they had been with Jesus.

Now when they saw the boldness of Peter and John, and perceived that they were uneducated, common men, they were astonished. And they recognized that they had been with Jesus.
Acts, Chapter 4, Verse 13 {ESV}

May our significance in this world be known in this respect that we have been with Jesus.
Jesus can take people, whether educated or uneducated, and give them a boldness to fulfil their ministry for God and be significant for Him for His glory alone.
And we can ready ourselves by spending time with the Lord in His Word.

The MSG – just to finish off the passage in the paraphrase:

V.14-16 No prolonged infancies among us, please. We'll not tolerate babes in the woods, small children who are an easy mark for impostors. God wants us to grow up, to know the whole truth and tell it in love—like Christ in everything. We take our lead from Christ, who is the source of everything we do. He keeps us in step with each other. His very breath and blood

flow through us, nourishing us so that we will grow up healthy in God, robust in love.
Ephesian 4.16-17 {MSG}

A Divine Mission

Are you catching the vision?

Catch the vision!

Get your ministry!

Get on your mission!

Yes you have a divine mission on earth.

Find your mission even if it is mission impossible!

You will succeed if God is in it!

Jesus said to the Father – Thy will be done!

We need to do the same – Father help me to find your will for my life and do it.

Father thy will be done in my life.

By Divine Means

Walk the Divinely chosen path and live by His resources!

All the resources of God are yours in Christ!

By Divine Motivation

Let the motion of the Holy Spirit move and motivate you! The human spirit is willing but the flesh is weak.

We can do all things through Him who gives us the strength. Paul could say:

> I have strength for all things through Him who strengthens me!
> Philippians, Chapter 4, Verse 13 {Berean Literal Bible}

I have just recently purchased a new version of the Bible and it's the LSV – The Literal Standard Version. And this is the rendering of Phil 4.13:

I have strength for all things, in Christ's strengthening me.

That is a beautiful rendering of that verse.

Paul was totally clear and absolutely convinced in his heart, mind and soul that God had called him to a specific ministry and work.

Likewise, God has a specific ministry and work for each of us to do.

Seek it, find it and do it.

We have a Divine Master who has a mighty mission for each of us.

We need to find out what it is and like Paul, just do it.

This is what kept Paul going in the face of tremendous persecution and constant danger –

He was called by God so giving up was not in his vocabulary.
It need not be in ours either.

> *Go labour on; spend, and be spent,*
> *Thy joy to do the Father's will;*
> *It is the way the Master went,*
> *Should not the servant tread it still?*
> *Horatius Bonar (1808-1889)*

We now move on from the first five verses, what we have entitled Paul's Sovereign Appointment, to verses 6-10.

V6-10. Paul's Serious Astonishment

V6. I am astonished that you are so quickly deserting him who called you in the grace of Christ and are turning to a different gospel—

V7. not that there is another one, but there are some who trouble you and want to distort the gospel of Christ.

V8. But even if we or an angel from heaven should preach to you a gospel contrary to the one we preached to you, let him be accursed.

V9. As we have said before, so now I say again: If anyone is preaching to you a gospel contrary to the one you received, let him be accursed.

V10. For am I now seeking the approval of man, or of God? Or am I trying to please man? If I were still trying to please man, I would not be a servant of Christ.

The Galatians were in danger!
They had found real freedom in Jesus Christ. Freedom from sin, freedom from their old life, freedom to serve Jesus Christ. Freedom purchased by the blood of Christ. They had been set free and now that freedom was threatened. It was threatened by people who wanted to drag them back to the past and away from the Gospel of grace; from freedom in Christ.
A different gospel was afoot indeed it was not another Gospel – it was anti-gospel. It was the very antithesis of the Good News of Jesus Christ.

V6. And Paul is astonished at them. For him it was beyond belief, if you pardon the pun.

Peterson paraphrases the verses in this way in the Message Bible:

V6-9. I can't believe your fickleness—how easily you have turned traitor to him who called you by the grace of Christ by embracing a variant message! It is not a minor variation, you know; it is completely other, an alien message, a no-message, a lie about God. Those who are provoking this agitation among you are turning the Message of Christ on its head.
{MSG: The Message Bible}

In these verses we see:

Disappointment
Paul could not take in how quickly they had turned away from the true gospel.
If Paul was writing a letter to us today would he be disappointed? I am aware we keep saying 'Paul said it' and we say it because Paul wrote it back then. But we need to be reminded that Paul was inspired by the Holy Spirit to write.

You could write something and feel inspired but that is not what we mean. The doctrine of the inspiration of Scripture is a whole different league. This is the Word of God – these are the words of God.

So the letter is written to every generation and therefore to our generation – to us. To us today.

It is written as a warning and it is written as a rebuke if it applies. If anyone is beginning to veer away from the true gospel of Jesus Christ.

And you can be sure in every generation and on every continent and in every country and in every group there will be the hand of the enemy sowing corrupt seed to seek to undermine and to destroy the true unadulterated Gospel of Jesus Christ. All the more reason to be in the Word and test the spirits to see if they are of God.

It is written for today because it is the infallible Word of God which Paul was inspired by the Holy Spirit to write. And these Scriptures were written to every generation as there will be those who will seek to hoodwink us and take us away from the true Gospel.

There will always be those who want to confuse people and to pervert the true Gospel of Jesus Christ. In his other letters Paul usually offers thanksgiving for the church. In this letter he goes straight to the heart of the very problem and does not beat about the bush – no mincing of words and rightly so because they were deserting the true Gospel and hence they were removing themselves from the very one who had called them – Jesus Christ.

In verse 8 we are told that if we or an angel from heaven were to preach any other gospel other than the one that was preached, that one should be accursed.

It may well be and some have conjectured that the exponents of this new gospel, rather, a perversion of the true Gospel could have been claiming their teaching had been revealed to them by angels. Sound familiar?

Secret mysteries unfolded to them by special angelic beings. Sound familiar? When people start saying that they have been given some special revelation we should not take their word for it but scrutinise it from the Divine benchmark of Scripture – if it is not in keeping with the Word of God then bin it. Test the spirits! And test them again and again!

In short, the false message was that works were necessary for salvation. The truth of the Gospel is that it is free and it's all of grace and it's God's gift of His beloved Son. We put our faith in Christ and

His finished work on the cross alone. Not our works. However, works are the outworking of His gift of salvation because we want to please Him. We work not to be saved because we are saved!

Faith comes by hearing and hearing by the word of God.
Romans 10.17 {NKJV}

We need to listen to the Word of God and when people tell us what we should do we need to go to the benchmark of the word of God. We need to be people of The Book. One Book, the Bible.
Why do you think the rulers of Israel were told to keep the Law of the Lord beside them? They were told, as was Joshua:

This Book of the Law shall not depart out of thy mouth; but thou shalt meditate therein day and night, that thou mayest observe to do according to all that is written therein: for then thou shalt make thy way prosperous, and then thou shalt have good success.
Joshua, Chapter 1, Verse 8 {KJV}

You can track down the pages of history and you will find that every nation and every individual who departed from the Word of God ended up in confusions and perversions of some kind or another. You only have to read in this book of God the history of the Children of Israel and you will see the consequences of departing from the Scriptures and the true Gospel.

Yes, the true Gospel. We look back to the cross and those in the Old Testament looked forward. The God of the Old Testament is the God of the New Testament.

> Turn to me and be saved,
> all the ends of the earth!
> For I am God, and there is no other.
> By myself I have sworn,
> from my mouth has gone out in righteousness
> a word that shall not return:
> To me every knee shall bow,
> every tongue shall swear allegiance.
> Isaiah, Chapter 45, Verses 22 and 23 {ESV}

Sound familiar – read Philippians Chapter 2. Jesus said:

V14. And as Moses lifted up the serpent in the wilderness, so must the Son of Man be lifted up, **15** that whoever believes in him may have eternal life.

16 For God so loved the world, that he gave his only Son, that whoever believes in him should not perish but have eternal life.

And what did Moses know about this Gospel?

> And behold, two men were talking with him, Moses and Elijah, who appeared in glory and spoke of his departure, which he was about to accomplish at Jerusalem.
> Luke, Chapter 9, Verses 30-31 {ESV}

And one more verse before we move on:

> And all drank the same spiritual drink. For they drank from the spiritual Rock that followed them, and the Rock was Christ.
> 1 Corinthians, Chapter 10, Verse 4 {ESV}

Jesus is the Rock of our Salvation and this is the one that the Galatians were deserting. The God of their Salvation.

Desertion

We are in a battle and the enemy of Souls seeks to pervert the true Gospel.

Let us not be on the AWOL deserter list of the Lord's Army but rather on the side of truth and right and Jesus Christ no matter what cost or the sacrifice.

This Gospel is written in blood! In the blood of Jesus Christ our Lord – it was not cheap so don't sell it cheap, for that which is not a gospel but only the rantings of ignorant minds dressed up in garments of so-called intelligence and worldly wisdom inspired by the influences of the Devil.

There is more than a tendency today to put Self on the throne and proclaim that I know better than my forefathers who split their blood for the cause of Jesus Christ. The martyrs were burned at the stake, now some of those who would deign to occupy the same positions and indeed the very same pulpits would rather burn the Bible than have it read. Albeit a metaphorical burning – a burning in the fires of higher criticism and so-called 21st century enlightenment.

We need to get back to the Bible! It is the Word of God.

It was the same spirit abroad in the days of Jeremiah when God in His great mercy and longsuffering to a wayward and rebellious people called out through His prophet:

> This is what the LORD says: "Stop at the crossroads and look around. Ask for the old, godly way, and walk in it. Travel its path, and you will find rest for your souls. But you reply, 'No, that's not the road we want.'
> Jeremiah, Chapter 6, Verse 16 {NLT}

> Isaiah also had similar words to say:
> And an highway shall be there, and a way, and it shall be called The way of holiness; the unclean shall not pass over it; but it shall be for those: the wayfaring men, though fools, shall not err therein.
> Isaiah, Chapter 35, Verse 8 {NKJV}

This true Gospel proclaims Jesus Christ as the Way, the Truth and the Life – the One who gave Himself for our sins to set us free from the present evil age. The One who died that we might live and lives that we might never die because he rose again from the dead.

Difference
Paul says they were turning from the true Gospel to a different gospel.

Distortion
And yet it was not a different gospel at all – there is only one true Gospel. Paul says not that there is another gospel!

The Gospel of Jesus Christ is a Gospel of Grace. Because:

For by grace you have been saved through faith, and that not of yourselves; *it is* the gift of God, not of works, lest anyone should boast.
Ephesians, Chapter 2, Verses 8 and 9 {NKJV}

Danger
The faith communities were in danger – so Paul writes to warn them and to get them off the slippery slopes of unbelief and salvation by works.

Damnation
There is only one Gospel – The True Gospel is our only safe and solid ground.

Redemption ground the ground of peace.
Redemption ground Oh wondrous grace.
Oh let our praise to God abound,
Who saves us on redemption ground.

Declaration

And this is no light matter! Paul states that for anyone to tinker about or play about with or modify or distort or manufacture a different Gospel – he wants that one to be accursed – anathema – and he uses a double curse for emphasis.

Distinction

The Gospel of Jesus Christ is distinctive and stands above and apart from all others. Jesus Christ is the only way to God and it's all of grace. You can't earn it. You can't buy it. You are a sinner and you need to rely solely on the finished work of Christ for salvation and trust in Him as your Saviour and Lord. Paul was indeed astonished that the Galatians could be so foolish as to move from a position of unconditional acceptance by God through His Son's sacrifice for sin to a conditional position, where they had to do certain things to merit this costly and free salvation. Which is totally impossible.

The lyrics of Augustus Montague Toplady's hymn Rock of Ages capture this for us.

> *Not the labors of my hands*
> *Can fulfil thy law's commands;*
> *Could my zeal no respite know,*
> *Could my tears forever flow,*
> *All for sin could not atone;*
> *Thou must save, and thou alone.*
> *Nothing in my hand I bring,*
> *Simply to the cross I cling;*
> *Naked, come to thee for dress;*
> *Helpless, look to thee for grace;*
> *Foul, I to the fountain fly;*
> *Wash me, Savior, or I die.*

The hymn is Rock of Ages and it was written in 1776 and based on Deuteronomy 32, verses 3-4, and Isaiah 26, Verse 4.

> Because I will publish the name of the LORD: ascribe ye greatness unto our God. He is the Rock, his work is perfect: for all his ways are judgment: a God of truth and without iniquity, just and right is he.
> Deuteronomy, Chapter 32, Verses 3-4 {KJV}

Trust ye in the Lord for ever: for in the Lord Jehovah is everlasting strength.
Isaiah, Chapter 32, Verse 4. {KJV}

Demarcation

There is a clear line of demarcation drawn and it separates those who trust in Christ alone and know that their own righteousnesses are as filthy rags in the sight of a Holy God, and those who think they know better and rely on works.

Defence

Paul defends the pure unchanging gospel and in every generation the people of God are called to do so. As we fast near the end of the world it's even more imperative that we defend the true Gospel.

One study recently published found that a majority of people who described themselves as 'American Christians' accepted a works-oriented means to God's acceptance.

The study conducted by the Culture Research Center at Arizona Christian University found that 48% of adults believed that if a person is generally good or does enough good things during their life then they will earn a place in heaven.

This is December 2020 – the year of the Covid-19

pandemic. Here is a much greater pandemic, the pandemic of heresy and the jettisoning of the true Gospel.

Another study found that the majority of so-called Christians did not believe that Jesus Christ is God.

The Bible says that to preach any other Gospel, that person is to be accursed – anathema!

Desire

The desire of the inspired writer and the Divine Inspirer is to present the truth and expose serious and damnable error.

Doulos

As the servants – the bond slaves of Christ let us defend the True Gospel.

Let's pray for our nation to get back to the Word and let's get the people we know to get into the Word of God.

Let's do what Philip did. It's worth repeating! He was led by the Spirit to that man who in Acts Chapter 8 was reading from Isaiah the Prophet in his chariot. We are told that he was reading the passage; He was led as a sheep to the slaughter and like a lamb before her shearers is dumb, so He opened not His mouth.

And we are told in verse 35 then Philip opened his mouth, and began at the same Scripture, and preached unto him Jesus.

The world needs Jesus. You need Jesus and I need Jesus!

The Gospel that Paul preached is exactly the same Gospel that we need to proclaim today.

The pure unadulterated Gospel of Christ.

Salvation is in Christ alone by faith alone.

The Gospel of God is totally exclusive. There is but one Gospel. There is but one way to God.

> And there is salvation in no one else, for there is no other name under heaven given among men by which we must be saved.
> Acts 4:12 {ESV}

> The Gospel of God is both exclusive and inclusive.
> It is one way, the only way to God open to all.
> For "everyone who calls on the name of the Lord will be saved."
> Romans 10:13 {ESV}

Paul sought the approval of God, not the approval of people. His priority and mission was to be a Servant (Doulos of Christ).

Seeking the approval of people for him was tantamount to relinquishing his status as the servant of Christ.

The reality is it's the same for us. Pleasing God should be our priority constantly as the servants of Christ.

And how do we know how to please Him? We know from reading His Word and hearing His Voice therein.

> And your ears shall hear a word behind you, saying, "This is the way, walk in it," when you turn to the right or when you turn to the left.
> Isaiah 30.21 {ESV}

We now turn to verses 11-24.

V11-24 Paul's Sovereign Assignment

Here are three alternative headings to the first chapter.

V1-5 Greetings and Grace
V6-10 Dissertation and Distortion
V11-24 God and His Gospel
V11-24 Paul's Sovereign Assignment

V11. For I would have you know, brothers, that the gospel that was preached by me is not man's gospel.

V12. For I did not receive it from any man, nor was I taught it, but I received it through a revelation of Jesus Christ.

V13. For you have heard of my former life in Judaism, how I persecuted the church of God violently and tried to destroy it.

V14. And I was advancing in Judaism beyond many of my own age among my people, so extremely zealous was I for the traditions of my fathers.

V15. But when he who had set me apart before I was born, and who called me by his grace,

V16. was pleased to reveal his Son to me, in order that I might preach him among the Gentiles, I did not immediately consult with anyone;

V17. nor did I go up to Jerusalem to those who were apostles before me, but I went away into Arabia, and returned again to Damascus.

V18. Then after three years I went up to Jerusalem to visit Cephas and remained with him fifteen days.

V19. But I saw none of the other apostles except James the Lord's brother.

V20. (In what I am writing to you, before God, I do not lie!)

V21. Then I went into the regions of Syria and Cilicia.

V22. And I was still unknown in person to the churches of Judea that are in Christ.

V23. They only were hearing it said, "He who used to persecute us is now preaching the faith he once tried to destroy."

V24. And they glorified God because of me.

V11-24 Paul's Sovereign Assignment
(V11-24 God and His Gospel)

The Gospel of God
Its Origination

Paul asserts that the Gospel that he preached is not man's gospel.

Indeed this is his defence of the Gospel that he proclaimed and he makes it clear that it was not of human origin. It was not a man-made message. It was not the result of human intelligence or human invention. Indeed the message does not equate with human wisdom at all and stands in direct antithesis to it. What do I mean? Let me put it this way; how can a man dying on a cross over two thousand years ago save my soul and redeem me from the slave market of sin and deliver me from the final consequence of sin which is a lost, undone eternity, the damnation of hell forever?

It's certainly not of human origin.

Paul reinforces his argument by saying that he did not receive it from any human source whatsoever but rather he received it through the revelation of Jesus Christ.

Paul had a Damascus road conversion. It was more than dramatic!

Paul gives a little bit of his testimony of what happened to him. The Galatians knew all about his conversion. As a zealous Jew he was fanatical about his beliefs and he was diametrically opposed to the Church of Jesus Christ; so much so that he, in his own words in verse 13 said that beyond measure he persecuted the Church of God, and wasted it. That is, he sought to destroy it. Every waking moment was given over to his one priority to obliterate the Church of Jesus Christ. What intense hatred!

Vivid language is also used in Acts by Dr. Luke.

> But Saul, still breathing threats and murder against the disciples of the Lord, went to the high priest and asked him for letters to the synagogues at Damascus, so that if he found any belonging to the Way, men or women, he might bring them bound to Jerusalem.
> Acts, Chapter 9, Verses 1 and 2 {ESV}

Paul consented to the death of the first Christian martyr. He was an accessory to the crime.

Paul stated:

> And when the blood of Stephen your witness, was being shed, I myself was standing by and approving and watching over the garments of those who killed him.
> Acts, Chapter 22, Verse 10 {ESV}

This was a man you would not want to meet if you were a Christian in his pre-conversion days.

But then the road to Damascus happened.

And what happened?

Paul encountered the Lord Jesus Christ.

In his own words:

> But when God, who had set me apart before I was born and called me through his grace, was pleased to reveal his Son to me, so that I might proclaim him among the Gentiles, I did not confer with any human being.
>
> Verses 15, 16 {NRSV}

This man was confronted with Jesus Christ. He turned his life over to the Lord Jesus and he was born again and his life was never the same again. He went down the Damascus road bound in sin and nature's night and he came off the road to destruction as a new person in Christ and in the freedom that only the Savour can give.

He then tells us what happened in relation to eventually meeting Peter and James and others. He says:

> Then I went into the regions of Syria and Cilicia, and I was still unknown by sight to the churches of Judea that are in Christ; they only heard it said, "The one who formerly was persecuting us

is now proclaiming the faith he once tried to destroy." And they glorified God because of me. Verses 21-24 {NRSV}

Paul's conversion occurred by being brought face to face with Jesus Christ. As a direct result of Divine intervention Paul was stopped abruptly on the road to Damascus and confronted with Jesus Christ and his life was changed in a moment and he became a proclaimer of the faith that he once sought to waste!

He was now a follower of Jesus and Jesus became his Lord and Master. He would now walk a different road, in a different direction with a new motivation – to serve the living Christ to the end of his days, whatever the cost involved.

He wrote the following words to the Philippians:

Furthermore, I count everything as loss compared to the possession of the priceless privilege, the overwhelming preciousness, the surpassing worth, and supreme advantage of knowing Christ Jesus my Lord and of progressively becoming more deeply and intimately acquainted with Him, of perceiving and recognizing and understanding Him more

fully and clearly. For His sake I have lost everything and consider it all to be mere rubbish, refuse, dregs, in order that I may win - gain - Christ , He Anointed One).
Philippians, Chapter 3, Verses 7-8 {AMP}

And then he says this in verse 9 of that chapter, which fits exactly with what Paul says to the churches at Galatia:

And may be found in Him [believing and relying on Him], not having any righteousness of my own derived from [my obedience to] the Law and its rituals, but [possessing] that [genuine righteousness] which comes through faith in Christ, the righteousness which comes from God on the basis of faith.

The same grace that reached Paul on the road of Damascus and turned his life around is the same grace that avails today. The Gospel hasn't changed one iota and the Saviour hasn't changed either. For He is Jesus Christ - the same yesterday and today and for all ages.
Hebrews 13.8. {LSV}

He still comes to individuals on the road of life and calls us by his grace to follow Him – to have done with our past sins and our wayward, rebellious, sinful lives and own Him as Saviour and Lord. And live for Jesus Christ alone.

This is the true freedom that Paul is expounding in this inspired letter.

Its Revelation

It's a revelation – the Jesus he hated and detested he now loved and followed.

The Jesus we once despised we now worship and adore.

If He is not your Saviour and Lord this is your moment to embrace Him and hand your life over to Him.

Notice what Paul says:

Its Proclamation

But when God, who had chosen me and set me apart before I was born, and called me through His grace, was pleased to reveal His Son in me so that I might preach Him among the Gentiles [as the good news—the way of salvation], I did not immediately consult with anyone for guidance regarding God's

call and His revelation to me.
Verses 15,16 {AMP}

Now that is awesome! He declares that God had
chosen him and set him apart before he was born
for the purpose of not only saving him but using
him to preach the Gospel among the gentiles – the
very people he once tried to waste and destroy.
Paul who was one the pious fanatical pharisee now
preaching the free grace of God's salvation. And it's
free! And it spells freedom from the rags of empty
dead religion and pharicial hatred as well as
profligate lifestyles and living a mere existence
without God. Whether it's the clean side or the
dirty side of the broad road it's the same bondage
to sin and the same destination.
But the Gospel is free – it's for whosoever will may
come.

> And the Spirit and the bride say, Come. And let
> him that heareth say, Come: and let him that is
> athirst, come: and let whosoever will, take of
> the water of life freely.
> Revelation, Chapter 22, Verse 17 {GNV}

The Gospel must be proclaimed to everyone. It is for everyone to hear and heed. And at the same time we have like Paul been chosen before we were born.

The best commentary on the Bible is the Bible.

Listen to what Paul has to say to the church at Ephesus on these matters in relation to the mystery of His Will.

Praise be to the God and Father of our Lord Jesus Christ, who has blessed us in the heavenly realms with every spiritual blessing in Christ. For He chose us in Him before the creation of the world to be holy and blameless in his sight. In love He predestined us for adoption to sonship through Jesus Christ, in accordance with His pleasure and will— to the praise of His glorious grace, which He has freely given us in the One He loves. In Him we have redemption through His blood, the forgiveness of sins, in accordance with the riches of God's grace that He lavished on us. With all wisdom and understanding, He made known to us the mystery of His will according to His good pleasure, which He purposed in Christ, to be put into effect when the times reach their fulfilment—to bring unity to all things in heaven and on earth under Christ. In Him we were also chosen, having been predestined according to the plan of him who works out everything in conformity with the purpose of His will, in order that we, who were the first to put our hope in Christ, might be for the praise of His glory. And you also were included in Christ when you heard the message of truth, the gospel of your salvation. When you believed, you were marked in Him with a seal, the promised Holy Spirit, who is a deposit guaranteeing our inheritance until the redemption of those who are God's possession—to the praise of his glory.

Ephesians, Chapter 1, Verses 3-14 {AMP}

The famous American Bible teacher Donald Grey Barnhouse used the following illustration to help people make sense of the doctrine of election.

He asked them to imagine a cross like the one on which Jesus died, only so large that it had a door in it.

Over the door were these words from Revèlation: 'Whosoever will may come.' These words represent the free and universal offer of the Gospel. By God's grace, the message of salvation is for everyone. Every man, woman and child who will come to the cross is invited to believe in Jesus Christ and enter eternal life.

One the other side of the door a happy surprise awaits the one who believes and enters. For from the inside, anyone glancing back can see these words from Ephesians written above the door: 'Chosen in Christ before the foundation of the world.'

Election is best understood in hindsight, for it is only after coming to Christ that one can know whether one has been chosen in Christ.

Those who make a decision for Christ find that God made a decision for them in eternity past.

Today – it is your decision! It is your decision today! What is your decision today? You need to make sure you make the right decision? Today the decision is your responsibility!

> As it is said, "Today, if you hear his voice, do not harden your hearts as in the rebellion."
> Hebrews, Chapter 3, Verse 15 {ESV}

Its Opposition

We will hear more about this in chapter 2 because there will always be opposition to the true Gospel. And do you know why?

Because it is the Gospel of God to bring us back from the place of being spiritually dead to being spiritually alive.

In Romans Paul described it as such:

> Paul, a servant of Christ Jesus, called to be an apostle, set apart for the gospel of God,
> Romans, Chapter 1, Verse 1 {ESV}

The Gospel of God –

Brings Salvation
Brings Regeneration
Brings Transformation

Just look at the salvation and regeneration and transformation of Paul. And this can be your experience too!

Our purpose as believers is to inform. To transit the Gospel. To transmit the Gospel. To tell the Gospel. To transcribe the Gospel. To translate the Gospel. To live the Gospel.

To take the Gospel to the world. Our everyday world. The people in our world of influence. Ours is the proclamation and God's is the transformation.

Let's leave it to God to transform. God is in the business of transforming lives through His one and only Gospel.

His truth is transforming truth.
And all the glory is His and His alone.

Oh the love that drew salvation's plan
Oh the grace that brought it down to man
Oh the mighty golf that God is span
At Calvary.

CHAPTER 2

NO OTHER GRACE

V1-10 Paul's acceptance by the church
V11-14 Paul's accusation against Cephas
V15-21 Paul's assurance in Christ

V1-10 Paul's acceptance by the church
This part of the letter shows how Paul and the message he preached was given full endorsement by the Church in Jerusalem.

V1. Then after fourteen years I went up again to Jerusalem with Barnabas, taking Titus along with me.

V2. I went up because of a revelation and set before them (though privately before those who seemed influential) the gospel that I proclaim among the Gentiles, in order to make sure I was not running or had not run in vain.

V3. But even Titus, who was with me, was not forced to be circumcised, though he was a Greek.

V4. Yet because of false brothers secretly brought in—who slipped in to spy out our freedom that we have in Christ Jesus, so that they might bring us into slavery—

V5. to them we did not yield in submission even for a moment, so that the truth of the gospel might be preserved for you.

V6. And from those who seemed to be influential (what they were makes no difference to me; God shows no partiality)—those, I say, who seemed influential added nothing to me.

V7. On the contrary, when they saw that I had been entrusted with the gospel to the uncircumcised, just as Peter had been entrusted with the gospel to the circumcised

V8. (for he who worked through Peter for his apostolic ministry to the circumcised worked also through me for mine to the Gentiles),

V9. and when James and Cephas and John, who seemed to be pillars, perceived the grace that was given to me, they gave the right hand of fellowship to Barnabas and me, that we should go to the Gentiles and they to the circumcised.

V10. Only, they asked us to remember the poor, the very thing I was eager to do.

Paul is seeking to remind the Galatians that the Gospel is a Gospel of Grace. It is all of God's sovereign grace.

Salvation is a gift, not something that we can merit by doing good and by performing good works.

When we come to these verses we may, at first reading, wonder what point Paul is trying to make.

From the previous chapter we note that Paul had gone to Jerusalem three years after his conversion. He had spent three years in the vicinity of the Arabian desert.

When we had to attend exegesis classes at theological college we used to joke and ask the question – where was Paul for those three years? Why, he was at our college of course. We can smile at that. However, Paul spent three years at the feet of Jesus. The Lord was preparing him for his ministry.

Let us never think that time waiting is time wasted. God is never in a hurry. And very often we are asked to wait. We need to build into our busy lives times of waiting on God. The secret is in the waiting.

He had trained as a pharisee and he was an expert in Jewish law and all that went with it. He was an exceptionally gifted man with loads of abilities but here is the point – he needed to spend time with Jesus. Waiting upon the Lord.

We all need times of isolation and obscurity when we get alone with the Master to hear His voice and learn at His feet. And that is something we will need to do for the rest of our lives. It's a daily thing too. Spending time in the presence of the Lord to get to know Him better and to allow Him to mould us and make us and shape us and equip us for the tasks He has for us, just as He prepared Paul.

Now Paul says after fourteen years he went up to Jerusalem again. And this is so significant and it adds a lot of weight to his argument against the false teachers. Indeed I would go so far as to say that it sounds the death knell for their heretical argument.

There is some debate as to which passage of Scripture in Acts refers to this event. I am running with Acts Chapter 15 which refers to the Jerusalem Council. Check out the chapter for yourself.

We find that a man called Barnabus along with Paul was instructed by the church in Antioch to go up to Jerusalem because of a massive dispute that had broken out. Check out Barnabus too – he is a gem of a person and he and Paul went back a long way; in fact all the way to Paul's first visit to Jerusalem. It was Barnabus who introduced Paul to the Jerusalem Apostles. The disciples were afraid of him and did not believe that Paul was now a disciple of Jesus.

Some people had come from Judea and began to teach the Christians that – yes, you have guessed correctly – they taught that a doctrine of legalism and that salvation was by works. They taught:

> Unless you are circumcised according to the custom of Moses, you cannot be saved.
> Acts, Chapter 15, Verse 1 {NRSV}

And so Paul and Barnabus and some others were appointed to go to Jerusalem to meet with the Apostles and Elders to discuss this very matter.

So this was an extremely important meeting for the Church at this juncture in its early history. And we know that there were three speeches given at the meeting. You can read these for yourself. The important thing to note for our purposes here in the Galatian context is that Acts Chapter fifteen forms one of the most forthright defences of the Gospel of Salvation by grace alone in the Bible.

Peter gave the first speech, then Paul and Barnabus gave the second speech and lastly James, the leader of the Church at Jerusalem gave the third speech.

The Council of Jerusalem was an unequivocal endorsement of the message Paul had been preaching from the beginning of his ministry as an Apostle of Jesus Christ.

The whole leadership of the Church in Jerusalem, where the church actually started, validated the message that has been preached at the beginning in Acts Chapter two that salvation is by Grace alone, in Christ alone, by Faith alone.

Peter quoted from the Old Testament Scriptures on that great day when the Holy spirit came. Among the words that he proclaimed are these:

> And it shall come to pass that whoever calls upon the Name of the Lord shall be saved.
> Acts, Chapter 2, Verse 21 {NKJV}

As Peter preached on, the people were convicted. Dr. Luke records:

When they heard this, they were cut to the heart, and said to Peter and the rest of the apostles, men and brethren what shall we do?

Acts, Chapter 2, Verse 37 {NKJV}

The Greek language here means they were pierced – stabbed with great grief and great remorse. They came under deep piercing spiritual conviction.

That is the work of the Holy Spirit and it was greatly evidenced here. The people realised that they had sinned and they had killed the Messiah. And remember that we all had a hand in the death of Christ.

That's what Peter preached in Acts, Chapter 3, Verse 15.

And the Prince of life you killed, whom God raised from the dead, of which we are witnesses.

{LSV – Literal Standard Version}

{Just bought a copy of the LSV and I love it! Worth getting and it can be downloaded onto Kindle, etc.}

Do you know that WE killed the Prince of Life? It was your sins and mine that took the Saviour to Calvary. And like the crowd on the Day of Pentecost we cry out, what shall we do?

The answer was given by Peter on that day. It was the same message that all the Apostles preached. It's the same message that the council of Jerusalem ratified fourteen years after the conversion of Saul/Paul.

It's the same message that Paul was defending to the Galatians. It's the same message that we proclaim today. And this is Peter's reply to the crowd.

> Repent and be baptized every one of you in the name of Jesus Christ for the forgiveness of your sins, and you will receive the gift of the Holy Spirit. For the promise is for you and for your children and for all who are far off, everyone whom the Lord our God calls to himself.
>
> Acts, Chapter 2, Verses 38-39 {NKJV}

And with many other words he bore witness and continued to exhort them, saying save yourselves from this crooked generation. So those who received his word were baptized, and there were added that day about three thousand souls. And they devoted themselves to the apostles' teaching and the fellowship, to the breaking of bread and the prayers.

Acts, Chapter 2, Verses 40-42

Notice the response of about three thousand souls; they gladly received the word and they were baptised.

Those who repented and turned to the Lord Jesus Christ for salvation followed their Lord through the waters of baptism thus identifying with the Lord Jesus in His death, burial and resurrection.

They were baptised not for the remission of sins but because of the remission of sins. Baptism is an outward sign of an inward work.

We walk in newness of life when we come to know Christ. He doesn't just give us a new start in life but He gives us a brand new life to start with.

And then we are to grow in grace as we feed on the word of truth.

The first time Paul went up to Jerusalem he only met with Peter and James. This time he met the Leaders of the Church Council and they gave him the right hand of fellowship, thus accepting him and his work and ministry.

This would have made the readers sit up and take notice. The false teachers were not going to get it all their own way and lead the churches astray. What they were peddling was diametrically opposed to the Gospel that was proclaimed from the beginning and that which was endorsed by the early Church Leaders and the eyewitnesses of the Glory and Grace and Majesty of our Lord Jesus Christ.

Johnny was in the band. His mum was annoyed because everyone was out of step on the day of the big parade apart from wee Johnny.

Paul was telling them to get back into line and keep in step with the teachings of the true Gospel. They were out of step to put it mildly, even though misguidedly, they thought it was the others who needed to get in step.

Let's get on to the next section where Paul was not behind the door in confronting Peter himself. Not about his doctrinal stance but rather about his practice.

We all need to talk the talk and walk the walk and indeed walk the talk and be consistent.

Paul defends the true Gospel:

Some pointers for you to flesh out:
The Participants in the Gospel
The Presentation of the Gospel
The Proclamation of the Gospel
The Preservation of the Gospel

The Preciousness of the Gospel
The Propagation of the Gospel
The Power of the Gospel
The Partnership in the Gospel
The Priority of the Gospel

V11-14 Paul's accusation against Cephas

Sometimes it can be useful, as we have already discovered, to read a paraphrase on the bible passage.
Here is the Message Bible Paraphrase on verses 11-14.

Later, when Peter came to Antioch, I had a face-to-face confrontation with him because he was clearly out of line. Here's the situation. Earlier, before certain persons had come from James, Peter regularly ate with the non-Jews. But when that conservative group came from Jerusalem, he cautiously pulled back and put as much distance as he could manage between himself and his non-Jewish friends. That's how fearful he was of the conservative Jewish clique that's been pushing the old system of circumcision. Unfortunately, the rest of the Jews in the Antioch church joined in that hypocrisy so that even Barnabas was swept along in the charade.

But when I saw that they were not maintaining a steady, straight course according to the Message, I spoke up to Peter in front of them all: "If you, a Jew, live like a non-Jew when you're not being observed by the watchdogs from Jerusalem, what right do you have to require non-Jews to conform to Jewish customs just to make a favorable impression on your old Jerusalem cronies?"

This behaviour undermined the teaching that Peter and Paul and the Apostles preached; salvation is by grace alone through faith alone.

The best of men are only men at the best. We all make mistakes. Indeed when we come to Galatians Chapter 6, Paul tells us under the inspiration of the Holy Spirit how to deal with the person who had fallen short; overtaken in a fault.

Our behaviour can, especially if we are afraid of people, be contextualised depending on who we are with – situational ethics is not a good look for the Christian.

If we have a tendency to be people pleasers this can compound the problem and the inconsistencies in our behaviour can further undermine the true and consistent message of the Gospel.

Like Paul, our priority must be to please God.

How many times have you heard people say that Christians have put them off Christianity? Let us ensure that our walk consistently matches our talk.

And if Christians have put you off – look to Christ – He is altogether lovely and there is no flaw or fault or sin in Him. Let no one and nothing stop you from coming to know Jesus Christ as your Saviour and Lord. Let no one hinder you from going on with God and following after Him.

Who are you allowing to live rent free in your head? And impinge on your walk with God? Renew your mind in Christ and follow Him. He never lets us down.

Coming back to Peter who was challenged by Paul; I do like Peter though; when I think of my own failures and shortcomings; when I have been told 'you are a leper' by a fellow Christian and no one will want to know you – and I am at a loss what to do: Peter comes to mind – he was an impetuous man, of course, who made his own mistakes. But he got up and got on with it. And the Lord was gracious with Him.

Don't let the Devil drag your failures into today or even tomorrow when Jesus has dealt with them yesterday.

And when we do fail and we do in thought and word and deed often, let us keep short accounts with God, and give Him our hearts that He can rule and reign in us and enable us to enjoy the freedom that He bought for us on the cross of Calvary.

Acknowledge your sin and move on with God. And as for Peter, God used him and he can use us, more often in spite of us, not because of us.

To sum up this section:

Here are some more heads for you to flesh out if you would like to.

Criticism (constructive not callous)
Condemnation
Compromise
Confusion
Conformity
Clarity

V15-21 Paul's assurance in Christ

V15. We ourselves are Jews by birth and not Gentile sinners;

V16. Yet we know that a person is not justified by

works of the law but through faith in Jesus Christ, so we also have believed in Christ Jesus, in order to be justified by faith in Christ and not by works of the law, because by works of the law no one will be justified.

V17. But if, in our endeavor to be justified in Christ, we too were found to be sinners, is Christ then a servant of sin? Certainly not!

V18. For if I rebuild what I tore down, I prove myself to be a transgressor.

V19. For through the law I died to the law, so that I might live to God.

V20. I have been crucified with Christ. It is no longer I who live, but Christ who lives in me. And the life I now live in the flesh I live by faith in the Son of God, who loved me and gave himself for me.

V21. I do not nullify the grace of God, for if righteousness were through the law, then Christ died for no purpose.

Paul expresses his confidence in Christ and he says:

We are justified in Christ
We are crucified in Christ
We are sanctified in Christ
We are satisfied in Christ
We are glorified in Christ

Some further thoughts and some questions to consider:

Here are some further thoughts as we conclude our alliteration and remarks on Chapter two.

How do we take criticism when it is justified?
Wherein could we compromise the Gospel?
Are we causing confusion for others?
We need clarity and we need conformity not to the world or its culture but to the Gospel of God.

Free from the law oh happy condition
Jesus has bled and there is remission
Cursed by the law and bruised by the fall
Christ has redeemed us one for All

Let us not miss the glorious truth in verse 16 which tells us that we are declared righteous. We are declared righteous through faith from Jesus Christ.

We are not declared righteous by the works of law. We are justified, i.e. made righteous by faith in Christ. We believe in Christ Jesus to be justified by faith in Christ. We are not justified by works. We are dead men walking in the sense that we have died to self – to the old sinful life and we live a new transformed life because Christ lives in us. Freedom! It's all about Him who loved us and gave Himself for us. He had our sins imputed to Him on the cross and we have the righteousness of Christ imputed to us. God accepts us as if we have never sinned because we are clothed in the righteousness of Christ.

Jesus alone fulfilled the law and the prophets. No one else ever has or ever could. We rely on the life and death and resurrection of Jesus Christ our wonderful Saviour and Lord. Jesus said:

'Do not think I have come to abolish the Law and the Prophets; I have not come to abolish them but to fulfil them. For truly I say to you, until heaven and earth pass away, not an iota, not a dot, will pass from the Law until all is accomplished.

Matthew 5.17,18 {ESV}

The Gospel is our priority. Peter was sent to the Jews and Paul to the Gentiles. God has chosen us to go and propagate the Gospel.

Who does He have in mind for us to share His Gospel? We need to find out. Go into all the world, Jesus said.

Who is in our world and who is in our sphere of influence?

And how are we to propagate the gospel?

The Righteous Shall Live by Faith.

> For I am not ashamed of the gospel, for it is the power of God for salvation to everyone who believes, to the Jew first and also to the Greek.
> Roman 1.16 {ESV}

CHAPTER 3

NO OTHER GOLGOTHA

V1-9 The Cause of being bewitched
The need for a Radical Refocusing

Our Faith in Christ

V10-14 The Cure for the curse
The need for a Radical Redemption

Our Freedom in Christ

V15-29 The Condition for being justified
The need for a Radical Reclothing

Our Fashion in Christ

V1-9 The Cause of being bewitched
The need for a Radical Refocusing
Our Faith in Christ

V1. O foolish Galatians! Who has bewitched you? It was before your eyes that Jesus Christ was publicly portrayed as crucified.

V2. Let me ask you only this: Did you receive the Spirit by works of the law or by hearing with faith?

V3. Are you so foolish? Having begun by the Spirit, are you now being perfected by the flesh?

V4. Did you suffer so many things in vain—if indeed it was in vain?

V5. Does he who supplies the Spirit to you and works miracles among you do so by works of the law, or by hearing with faith -

V6. just as Abraham "believed God, and it was counted to him as righteousness"?

V7. Know then that it is those of faith who are the sons of Abraham.

V8. And the Scripture, foreseeing that God would justify the Gentiles by faith, preached the gospel beforehand to Abraham, saying, "In you shall all the nations be blessed."

V9. So then, those who are of faith are blessed along with Abraham, the man of faith.

The bewitching of the faith

Paul begins this section of the inspired Scriptures by calling a spade a spade.

Oh foolish Galatians!

The Greek word rendered 'foolish' here refers to not having an understanding – of being unwise. They hadn't really reasoned this though but had been bewitched by the false teachers.

The word rendered 'bewitched' comes from a word meaning to cast an evil spell. But this is only used in Galatians figuratively and has the concept of people being totally spellbound or captivated by the false messengers. Indeed this message had the power of appeal to the fallen nature.

How many people have you met who want to buy their way to God. To prove how good they are, to do certain good works and adhere to certain religious observances and rituals to make them right with God. It appeals to the proud heart and the arrogant mind.

The Galatians were being hoodwinked and they

needed to be admonished and shown the folly of this kind of thinking in the light of the Free Gospel of Grace.

The basis of the faith
The bedrock of our faith is the finished work of Christ and in coming to Christ and exercising faith in Him we rest on what He has done and we receive the Holy Spirit as a seal until the day of our redemption.

The beginning of the faith
It all begins with hearing the Gospel.

> Faith comes by hearing and hearing by the Word of God.
> Romans, Chapter 10, Verse 17 {NKJV}

> The Spirit Himself testifies with our spirit that we are God's children.
> Roman, Chapter 8, Verse 16 {NIV}

So Paul asks them:

V2,3. Let me ask you only this: Did you receive the Spirit by works of the law or by hearing with faith?

Are you so foolish? Having begun by the Spirit, are you now being perfected by the flesh?

Then in V6-9 Paul refers to Abraham who was justified by faith. So those who seek to be justified with God by performing acts of obligation in relation to the Jewish law are actually doing so in stark contrast to Abraham.

> Abraham is a role model for all who seek to be justified by God because just as Abraham believed God and it was reckoned to him as righteousness, so you see, those who believe are the descendants of Abraham.
>
> Galatians, Chapter 3, Verse 6-7 {NRSV}

The belittling of the faith

To believe otherwise is to belittle the faith and indeed to belittle the work of Christ. And as Paul has said at the conclusion of chapter 2:

> I do not make the grace of God void, for if righteousness is through the law - that Christ died in vain.
>
> Galatians, Chapter 2.21 {LSV}

The bedrock of the faith

The word of God – thus says the Lord.

The blessedness of the faith

We rest by faith in what the Lord has done. Oh the blessedness of this great biblical truth.

Naught have I gotten but what I received
Faith has bestowed it since I believed
Boasting excluded, pride I abase,
I'm only a sinner saved by Grace.

The true Gospel – the need for a radical refocusing

My faith looks up to thee,
Blest Lamb of Calvary,
Oh hear me when I pray,
Take all my sin away,
Oh may I from this day
Be wholly thine.

Some ideas for you to flesh out:

A radical refocusing of:
Our Faith

-    Christ alone is the Author of our salvation – not us!

Our Focus

- Focus on Christ and His finished work.

Our Freedom

- Is found in what Christ has done

Our Fullness

- Is found in Christ, not in anything we can do.

Our Forefathers

- Believed and it was counted to them as righteousness.

Our Faithfulness

- To the Book and the blood.

Our Family

- We are adopted into the family of God.

Our Following

- We follow Christ, not man.

Our Fellowship

- Our fellowship is with the Father and with His Son and the Holy Spirit.

Our Fortitude

- Is found in Him, not my works.

Who did this? Paul asks. Who bewitched you?

Whose influence are you under? Paul wants to know. And whose influence are we under? We are, we should be, we must be under the Influence of the Holy Spirit!

We who put our faith in Christ received the Holy Spirit. And we received Him by hearing with faith and not by works of the law.

We are children of faith, as Paul indicates at the end of this section in v9. We need the ministry of the Holy Spirit.

In this section we see the significance of the Holy Spirit in our lives.

The imparting of the Holy Spirit

In V2 Paul asks a very simple question but a very searching question:

The only thing I want to learn from you is this: did you receive the Spirit by doing the works of the law or by believing what you heard?

The indwelling of the Holy Spirit

The Holy Spirit is given to us at the moment of our conversion. We received Him when we believed.

And having received the Holy Spirit by faith in believing why would they be so foolish to have begun in the Spirit to then end with the flesh?

The influence of the Holy Spirit

Having been brought under the influence of the Holy Spirit and being guided and directed by Him, why would they elevate works to such an extent they were in danger of nullifying the influence of the Spirit upon their lives?

Just to make a point clear here, the Holy Spirit is a Person, not an influence. He is the Third Person of the Trinity and to be worshipped and adored. Jesus made the promise that He would send the Spirit to be with us and indwell us and we need to be under the control and influence of the Holy Spirit.

We need to walk in the Spirit.

If we walk in the Spirit we shall not fulfil the lusts of the flesh. We are under His influence and not the influences of the world, the flesh and the Devil.

The infusion of the Holy Spirit

And the Spirit empowers us – He infuses us with

power. Paul says that God supplies us with the Spirit {V5} and works miracles amongst the people of God. Now how does He do this?

Does He do it by the people of God doing the works of the law or does He do it by believing what we have heard? I.e. the Gospel of our Lord Jesus Christ. {V5}

And then the Scriptures tell us about Abraham. Abraham, as we have already noted, is the model for the Christian faith. Abraham was justified by faith. And he stands here in direct contrast to those who would teach that justification is achieved through performing the practices of the Jewish law.

That's a powerful argument for the Galatians to hear.

V6. Abraham believed God and it was accounted to him as righteousness. It was reckoned to him; it was imputed to him as righteousness.

This echoes the words of the Book of Genesis.

These are the words we read in the first book of the Bible.

> And he believed in the Lord; and He counted it to him as righteousness.
> Genesis, Chapter 15, Verse 6 {KJV}

And those who believe are descendants of Abraham.
Then he says something very wonderful. {V8} He tells us that way back then in the very first book of the Old Testament, the Book of Genesis, that God told Abraham about us, yes, the gentiles who would be the recipients of the Gospel by faith.
Indeed the Scriptures foreseeing that God would justify the gentiles by faith declared the Gospel beforehand to Abraham, saying All the gentiles shall be blessed in you.

> Now the Lord had said to Abram: "Get out of your country, From your family And from your father's house, To a land that I will show you. I will make you a great nation; I will bless you And make your name great; And you shall be a blessing. I will bless those who bless you, And I will curse him who curses you; And in you all the families of the earth shall be blessed."
> Genesis, Chapter 12, Verses 1-3 {NKJV}

Can you see how the Bible is its own interpreter?
Can you see how Galatians refers us back to Genesis and interprets it for us?
It has been estimated that the Bible has 63,779 direct cross-references. A cross reference is a

scripture that references another scripture. Some have estimated this as much higher and over 300,000 to be more accurate.

Oh how we need to read the Word.

Get a Bible that has cross-references and as you read, note these. Very often, particularly in the Gospels we find the words 'and so it was fulfilled' and then the writer under the influence of the Holy Spirit quotes the reference in the Old Testament.

So Paul tells us in Galatians Chapter 3 that God declared the Gospel beforehand to Abraham.

God's great plan of salvation declared unto Abraham. We need to be led by the Holy Spirit. And so the need to be in the inspired Word of God:

> Knowing this first of all, that no prophecy of Scripture comes from someone's own interpretation. For no prophecy was ever produced by the will of man, but men spoke from God as they were carried along by the Holy Spirit.
> 2, Peter, 1.20-21 {ESV}

Don't be bewitched!

We need in these days a radical refocusing on faith!

Faith in Christ alone for salvation! Just like Abraham!

V10-14 The Cure for the curse
The need for redemption
Our Freedom in Christ

When we think of Law what do we think of?
I tend to think of such things as obeying the speed limit, paying taxes and generally obeying the laws of our country. I write this in the middle of the Global Covid-19 pandemic and the Prime Minister is addressing the nation in one hour to tell the UK what the laws will be in relation to certain restrictions and the penalties that will be imposed upon us. For example, not adhering to self-isolation on returning from a quarantined destination will involve a very stiff monetary penalty indeed; some £10,000.

When I think of law I think of law and order. Good government does not impose laws for the sake of it but for the health and safety and wellbeing of society as a whole. So if a government made up of people who are human and who don't always get it right, sees fit to impose laws on its people, how much more attention should we give to the Law of the everlasting God which He gave to Israel through His Servant Moses?

Paul has a lot to say now about the Law of God –

let's look at what he has to say.

In Verse 10 we are told that those who rely on the works of the law are under a curse.

He has already told us in the earlier part of the chapter that they had received the Holy Spirit when they believed and were converted to Christ and not by doing the works of the law.

Paul then gives a quotation from the Old Testament and it comes from the book of obedience, Deuteronomy, Chapter 27, Verse 26.

Verse 10

For all who rely on works of the law are under a curse; for it is written, "Cursed be everyone who does not abide by all things written in the Book of the Law, and do them."

What does Paul mean?

He explains what he means in the next verse, Verse 11.

Clearly no one who relies on the law is justified before God, because "the righteous will live by faith."

In other words you cannot possibly be justified before a Holy God by keeping the law in its entirety.

It is obviously a good thing to seek to keep the law

of God and we will come back to this point shortly. But here is the thrust of what Paul is saying at this juncture; if you are depending on keeping the law of God to be accepted by God and to be justified by works that's impossible.

Rather, The just shall live by faith. And the quote is from Habakkuk, Chapter 2, Verse 4.

The one who is righteous will live by faith. {NRSV}

Here is true freedom. We are justified by faith. We live in the freedom that Christ has won for us on Calvary. Christ has redeemed us from the curse of the law having become a curse for us.

Here are some further headings for you to flesh out.

The condemnation of the law

No longer under condemnation!

The curse of the law

No longer under the curse!

The code of the law

No longer tortured by our consciences because we cannot keep the entire law of God perfectly.

The conditions of the law
No longer frustrated because we cannot fulfil the law of God!

The challenge of the law
No longer challenged by our failure to keep the law of God.

The consequences of the law
No longer a slave to fear because we will not suffer the consequences of our sinful nature and our ineptitude at trying to be what we cannot be.

The catalyst of the law
No longer looking to ourselves but looking to Christ!

The Christ and the law
Our Lord Jesus Christ is the only person who ever walked this planet who kept the law to perfection. The only one without sin.

The cross and the law
And so we rest in His accomplished redemption and we are accepted by the Father through His sinless Son.

The law does not rest on faith but on works.

> But Christ has redeemed us from the curse of the law by becoming a curse for us - for it is written, cursed is everyone who hangs on a tree. Deuteronomy, Chapter 21, Verse 23 {NRSV}

On Calvary's tree Jesus took our curse and we go free!

> The Law was our Schoolmaster to bring us to Christ, that we might be justified by faith. Galatians 3.24 {KJV}

Let the words sink in – Christ became a curse for us! He became an offering for sin once and for all. And thereby redeemed us from the curse.

On Christ Almighty vengeance fell
That would have sunk the world to hell
He bore it for a chosen race
And thus became my hiding place

We are free! We rest and we glory in the cross of our Lord Jesus Christ, not a wooden cross but the cross work of our Lord.

V14 So that in Christ Jesus the blessing of Abraham might come to the Gentiles, so that we might receive the promised Spirit through faith.

In John's Gospel we read:

> Jesus said, "Your Father Abraham rejoiced that he would see my day. He saw it and was glad."
> So the Jews said to him, "You are not yet fifty years old, and have you seen Abraham?" Jesus said to them, "Truly, truly, I say to you, before Abraham was, I am."
> John 8.56-58 {ESV}

The completion of the law

Jesus fulfilled the law and grace flows from Him to sinner and forgiveness is made possible for us who have broken God's law in thought and word and in deed.

And then Paul follows on with the implications of the finished work of Christ in verse 14.

In order that in Christ Jesus the blessing of Abraham might come to the gentiles, so that we might receive the promise of the Spirit through faith.

And so because of the finished work of Christ both Jew and gentile have freedom and can live in the

Spirit of God. Later on Paul tells us all about that in terms of the fruit of the Spirit.

So what about the law of God in the Old Testament? Is it abolished now? Is it rendered out of date and not relevant to persons of faith? After all, we are now free in Christ!

Well now the law of God tells us how to live – most people are familiar with the 10 commandments.

Joshua was told by God:

> This Book of the Law shall not depart from your mouth, but you shall meditate on it day and night, so that you may be careful to do according to all that is written in it. For then you will make your way prosperous, and then you will have good success.
>
> Joshua, Chapter 1, Verse 8 {ESV}

Now we know that we are not under law but under grace. And:

> Sin is no longer your master, for you no longer live under the requirements of the law. Instead, you live under the freedom of God's grace.
>
> Romans, Chapter 6, Verse 14 {NLT}

John tells us in his Gospel:

> For the law was given through Moses; grace and
> truth came through Jesus Christ.
> John, Chapter 1, Verse 17 {ESV}

We are not under law but under grace. But by the grace of God we will now seek to obey the law of God not to obtain justification but because we already have it and we live in the Spirit and we want to please God, and how best to do that but live by His revealed laws and ordinances and keeping His commands to do them.

And when we fail we don't go into a never-ending downward spiral of despair but rather we know we can look to the Perfect One.

When Satan tempts me to despair,
And tells me of the guilt within,
Upward I look and see Him there,
Who made an end of all my sin.
John wrote:

> My dear children, I am writing this to you so that
> you will not sin. But if anyone does sin, we have
> an advocate who pleads our case before the

Father. He is Jesus Christ, the one who is truly righteous.

First John, Chapter 2, Verse 1 {NLT}

Come Sing my Soul

Come sing, my soul, and praise the Lord,
Who hath redeemed thee by His blood;
Delivered thee from chains that bound,
And brought thee to redemption ground.
Refrain
Redemption ground, the ground of peace!
Redemption ground, O wondrous grace!
Here let our praise to God abound!
Who saves us on redemption ground.
Once from my God I wandered far,
And with His holy will made war;
But now my songs to God abound;
I'm standing on redemption ground.
Refrain
O joyous hour! when God to me
A vision gave of Calvary;
My bonds were loosed—my soul unbound;
I sang upon redemption ground.
Refrain
No works of merit now I plead,

But Jesus take for all my need;
No righteousness in me is found,
Except upon redemption ground.
Refrain
Come, weary soul, and here find rest;
Accept redemption, and be blest;
The Christ who died, by God is crowned
To pardon on redemption ground.
Refrain
(Daniel W Whittle 1840 - 1901)

And so having considered verses 10-14 – the Cure for the curse and the need for a radical redemption – true freedom.
We now move on to:

V15-29 The Condition of being justified
The need for a radical reclothing
Our Fashion in Christ

The Christian needs to be fashion conscious and put on Christ!

The promise to Abraham
In verses 14-18 Paul argues that the covenant blessing promised to Abraham was fulfilled in Jesus

Christ the Messiah.

The purpose of the law

The law came 430 years after Abraham and did not annul the covenant previously ratified by God. The inheritance does not come from the law but through the promise to Abraham. The purpose of the law is to bring us to Christ.

The law was given because of transgressions – and for Israel was a temporary means of discipline for the Israelites.

The person of Christ

V19 The law was in place until the Offspring i.e. Christ would come to whom the promise had been made.

The law did not oppose the promise of God.

V21. The law could not give life but showed all sinners for what we are – all have sinned and fallen short of God's glory, Paul wrote in Romans, Chapter 3, Verse 23. It is faith in Christ that obtains the promise of righteousness and acceptance with God.

V22. And before faith came we were under the condemnation of the law

V23. indeed the law was our Schoolmaster

V24 Or our disciplinarian until Christ came, so that we might be justified by faith. But now since faith has come we are no longer under the schoolmaster - the disciplinarian - the law. For;

V26. in Christ Jesus you are children of God through faith. And as many of you who have been baptised into Christ have clothed yourselves with Christ.

In Romans, Chapter 13, Verse 14, Paul says: Rather, clothe yourselves with the Lord Jesus Christ, and do not think about how to gratify the desires of the flesh.

V28. We are all one in Christ Jesus.

V29 and if we belong to Christ then are we Abraham's seed or Abraham's offspring and heirs according to the promise.

Christ saves us from our plight as sinners and

positions us in Himself, we are clothed in Him and we all are, Jew and Gentile alike, we are the progeny of Abraham.

We are to wear a new fashion. Not a fading fashion or a worldy fashion but the Jesus fashion.

Be like Jesus!
We are children of promise.

Children of the promise by Faith in Jesus Christ.
We are justified by faith.
Sons and daughters of God through faith.
We are the offspring of Abraham.
We are one in Christ.
We need to put on Christ.
We are clothed in the righteousness of Christ so we need to be righteous as He is righteous.
We don't do righteous to obtain righteousness, we do it because we have His righteousness imputed to us.

So wear it well.

Redemption
Justification
Sanctification

So our meditations on V15-29 – The Condition of being justified and the need for a radical reclothing – Our Fashion concludes chapter 3.

CHAPTER 4

NO OTHER GUARDIAN

V1-7 Converts as the Children of God
V8-20 Concerns for the Children of God
V21-31 Clarity for the Children of God

V1-7 Converts as the Children of God

V1. I mean that the heir, as long as he is a child, is no different from a slave, though he is the owner of everything,

V2. but he is under guardians and managers until the date set by his father.

V3. In the same way we also, when we were children, were enslaved to the elementary principles of the world.

V4. But when the fullness of time had come, God sent forth his Son, born of woman, born under the law,

V5. to redeem those who were under the law, so that we might receive adoption as sons.

V6. And because you are sons, God has sent the Spirit of his Son into our hearts, crying, "Abba! Father!"

V7. So you are no longer a slave, but a son, and if a son, then an heir through God.

V1-7 Converts as the Children of God

Paul further elaborates his point that all who are in Christ Jesus are heirs of the promise and as such we as believers are brought into our inheritance as the adopted children of God. God is now our Guardian Father. And we can address Him in the most intimate and loving terms as Abba! Father.
Prior to this we were no better than slaves. We were slaves to sin and had broken God's law. No matter how we tried to keep the law of God and came under the discipline and tutelage and governance and guardianship of God's law, we failed. No one can perfectly keep the Law of God.

As Paul has indicated in 3.24:

The Law was our Tutor or Schoolmaster to bring us to Christ that we might be justified by faith.

Indeed we are told that we were under enslavement to the beggarly elements of this world. We were to all intents and purposes slaves to sin and enslaved by the world. The NRSV translates this as the elemental spirits of the world. And as such the Bible teaches that:

> All of us also lived among them at one time, gratifying the cravings of our flesh and following its desires and thoughts. Like the rest, we were by nature deserving of wrath. {KJV Children of wrath} Ephesians. Chapter 2. Verse 3 {NIV}

Here are some alliterative notes for you to think about and to flesh out from Scripture about children of wrath. And if you have not yet come to Christ and experienced His blood wrought and blood bought redemption, then this is your present condition and I would implore you to turn to Jesus now before it is forever too late.

The children of Wrath

- **Infantile Children of Wrath**
- **Iniquitous Children of Wrath**
- **Insolent Children of Wrath**
- **Indifferent Children of Wrath**
- **Indisciplined Children of Wrath**

But all is not lost because of what Paul then says in verse 4. But oh, dear reader, listen to what comes next in Verse 4. Because:
Christ has regarded our helpless estate
And has shed His own blood for our souls.
We should savour every word here and the divine profundity of it all!

V4. But when the fullness of time had come, God sent His Son, born of a woman, born under the law,

V5. In order to redeem those who were under the law, so that we might receive the adoption of children.
Galatians, Chapter 4, Verses 4-5 {NRSV}

These verses are so wonderful for sinners to see and grasp and believe.

At the time that God had set in the history of the world, He sent forth His Son who was born of a woman, born under the law to REDEEM...

Let us consider this wonderful word and when we see what it means and the context in which it is set we will give God all the glory for redeeming us!

The Greek word used here is transliterated 'exagorazo' and is defined in the following way:

- To buy up fully out of the marketplace
- To buy away from
- To rescue from loss
- To ransom
- To purchase out of
- Redeem
- Choose
- To redeem by the payment of a price
- To recover from the power of another

Jesus Christ our Lord has freed us from the power of sin and the dominion of the mosaic law at the price of His vicarious death. Peter reminds us:

V18. For you know that it was not with perishable things such as silver or gold that you were redeemed from the empty way of life handed down to you from your ancestors,

V19. but with the precious blood of Christ, a Lamb without blemish or defect.

1, Peter 1, 18-19 {NIV}

The blood of Jesus is redeeming blood.
There is power in the blood of the Lamb.

- It is powerful blood
- It is precious blood
- It is pardoning blood
- It is perfect blood
- It is perfecting blood

And what did Jesus do for us?
He came right down to the slave market of sin.
He purchased us out of the slave market of sin.
He set us free from the slave market of sin.
He purchased us with His own precious blood.

This reminds me of the story I heard as a child that really helped me to grasp the concept of redemption. It struck me because I used to sail my little boat in Ward Park in Bangor, Co. Down, every morning on my summer holidays. Once I nearly lost the little boat that was my pride and joy so this story really resonated with me.

John loved to sail his little boat after school every day. One day he carried his pride and joy to the usual spot and carefully placed it in the water and slowly let out the string. It was a lovely day and the sun was shining bright. And the boat was sailing as smoothly as ever. The boat sailed! He was full of admiration and joy because he had crafted the little boat along with his father who was a boat builder. John loved that little boat.

All of a sudden a strong current caught the boat, the string broke and the boat went off downstream and raced away at the mercy of the powerful current.

John took to his heels and ran as fast as he could but alas, the boat soon disappeared from sight. He searched and searched and searched until dark but he could not find it. He went home sad and forlorn.

Some days later John was passing the village second-hand shop when he spotted a boat that looked very similar to the one he had lost. He stopped and looked more intently to see this boat. He got closer and he could not believe his very eyes – sure enough – it was his very own boat, the one he had made!

John rushed into the shop and spoke with great excitement to the shop assistant, "That's my boat in the window! I made that boat!"

"Sorry," said the shop assistant, "but that boat was brought in here the other day and if you want it, you will have to buy it."

John looked at the price tag and immediately ran home and counted all the money he had saved. He had the exact amount to pay for it.

He rushed back to the shop. "Here's the money for my boat."

As he walked home with his boat John held it tight and said, "Now you're twice mine. First I made you, and now I bought you."

And that, my dear friend, is redemption! – Bought back.

He who made us has bought us back and it cost God His dearest and best. He paid the price of our redemption with His own blood.

Can you say I am redeemed? Jesus is my Redeemer! It's time to come home from the lostness of where you are for He has made a way and He longs to embrace you and say I love you, you are mine!

Redeemed how I love to proclaim it,
Redeemed by the Blood of the Lamb,
Redeemed through His infinite mercy,
His child and forever I am!

And so Christ has redeemed us and made a way back to God the Father so we are His adopted children.
There is no other ground but redemption ground! Redemption is found in Christ alone!

V6. And because you are children, God has sent the Spirit of His Son into our hearts crying Abba! Father!

V7. So you are no longer a slave but a child, and if a child then an heir, through God.

Let us just stop there and allow ourselves to reflect on this. We are children of God by virtue of the redemption of Christ and our faith in Him and His finished work!

Here are some thoughts for you to think about and to flesh out in your own precious time as you meditate on the Word of God.

We are the Children of God

- **Ingrafted Children of God**
- **Integrated Children of God**

- **Indwelt Children of God**
- **Intimate Children of God**
- **Imitating Children of God**
- **Indebted Children of God**
- **Inspired Children of God**

Children?

> "Truly, I say to you, unless you turn and become like children, you will never enter the kingdom of heaven."
>
> Matthew, Chapter 18, Verse 3 {ESV}

We who were once children of wrath have become the Children of God.

V3. Among whom we all once lived in the passions of our flesh, carrying out the desires of the body and the mind, and were by nature children of wrath, like the rest of mankind.

V4. But God, being rich in mercy, because of the great love with which he loved us,

V5. even when we were dead in our trespasses, made us alive together with Christ—by grace you

have been saved...
Ephesians, Chapter 2, Verses 3-5 {ESV}

We are the family of God by virtue of Christ's redeeming work. Brothers and sisters in Christ Jesus. We can call God 'Abba' – Father.

We are in a relationship with Him and this ought to be an intimate relationship.

We now move on to verses 8-20 which I have entitled 'concerns for the children of God'.

V8-20 Concerns for the Children of God

V8. Formerly, when you did not know God, you were enslaved to those that by nature are not gods.

V9. But now that you have come to know God, or rather to be known by God, how can you turn back again to the weak and worthless elementary principles of the world, whose slaves you want to be once more?

V10. You observe days and months and seasons and years!

V11. I am afraid I may have labored over you in vain.

V12. Brothers, I entreat you, become as I am, for I also have become as you are. You did me no wrong.

V13. You know it was because of a bodily ailment that I preached the gospel to you at first,

V14. and though my condition was a trial to you, you did not scorn or despise me, but received me as an angel of God, as Christ Jesus.

V15. What then has become of your blessedness? For I testify to you that, if possible, you would have gouged out your eyes and given them to me.

V16. Have I then become your enemy by telling you the truth?

V17. They make much of you, but for no good purpose. They want to shut you out, that you may make much of them.

V18. It is always good to be made much of for a good purpose, and not only when I am present with you,

V19. my little children, for whom I am again in the

anguish of childbirth until Christ is formed in you!

V20. I wish I could be present with you now and change my tone, for I am perplexed about you.

Some headings or straplines to get us started!
Read over this section and notice some of the things we discover here.

V8-11. It's elementary really!

V9. Why would they turn back?

The enslavement of the past
V9. The past is about enslavement – bondage!
Why would anyone go back to that?

The experiential privileges of the saint
V9. To know God and to be known by Him!
What a privilege – but then to turn back.
The Devil wants us to turn back. He will use whatever he can to get us to turn back.
Don't turn back, the Scriptures say!
Who would leave the place of freedom for the place of bondage?

The endangerment that always exists
Satan wants to obliterate us – wipe us out!

In 1 Corinthians, Chapter 10, Paul speaks about the idolatry of the children.

Yes – the children of Israel in the wilderness. And oh, how privileged they were! God had brought them out of Egypt.

God had redeemed them!

And as we travel through the wilderness of this world we are told in that chapter to take heed of them in their wilderness wanderings. They serve as a warning to us. These who drank of that spiritual Rock that went with them and that Rock was Christ.

Yet how mighty was their fall. And Paul catalogues some of the terrible things they had indulged in and then he says this:

> These things happened to them to serve as an example, and they were written down to instruct us, on whom the ends of the ages have come. So if you think you are standing, watch out that you do not fall.
>
> Corinthians, Chapter 10, Verses 11-12 {NRSV}

And if the ends of the ages had come upon them,

how much more are we near the very end of the ages!

The elementary principles of the world

Let us not return to these beggarly things but rather put on the Lord Jesus Christ.

The emancipating power of God

God had ransomed them by His Power. And it's the power of the cross!

The enemy for expressing the truth

V16. Paul says, have I become your enemy, because I tell you the truth?

The explicit problem in the church

They were being influenced by the wrong people – people who were opposed to the true Gospel and the True Guardian of their souls.

Be careful therefore who you are influenced by!

The exclusion tactics of the enemy

V17. They zealously affect you, but not well;

V17,18. The false teachers had their hidden agenda and they wanted to exclude these believers for what they could get out of them.

The expressed perplexity of the Apostle

V19. Paul was perplexed for them. He describes it as akin to the pains of childbirth.

V20. How I wish I could be with you now and change my tone, because I am perplexed about you! {NIV}

We know God. God knows us. He knows everything about us. How well do we know Him? And if we know God how can we turn back?

To leave the place of blessedness to return to the place of barrenness. May Christ be truly formed in us. I.e., be fully developed in us. Not infantile or regressed but mature and progressing.

> *I'm pressing on the upward way,*
> *New heights I'm gaining every day,*
> *Though some may dwell where these are found,*
> *I must go on to higher ground.*

Oh how we need clarity and here it is for the Galatians and for us!

V21-31 Clarity for the Children of God

V21. Tell me, you who desire to be under the law,

do you not listen to the law?

V22. For it is written that Abraham had two sons, one by a slave woman and one by a free woman.

V23. But the son of the slave was born according to the flesh, while the son of the free woman was born through promise.

V24. Now this may be interpreted allegorically: these women are two covenants. One is from Mount Sinai, bearing children for slavery; she is Hagar.

V25. Now Hagar is Mount Sinai in Arabia; she corresponds to the present Jerusalem, for she is in slavery with her children.

V26. But the Jerusalem above is free, and she is our mother.

V27. For it is written,
"Rejoice, O barren one who does not bear;
break forth and cry aloud, you who are not in labor!
For the children of the desolate one will be more
than those of the one who has a husband."

V28. Now you, brothers, like Isaac, are children of promise.

V29. But just as at that time he who was born according to the flesh persecuted him who was born according to the Spirit, so also it is now.

V30. But what does the Scripture say? "Cast out the slave woman and her son, for the son of the slave woman shall not inherit with the son of the free woman."

V31. So, brothers, we are not children of the slave but of the free woman.

Paul says
Listen to the Word of promise

Paul says, do you not listen to the Law?

V21. Tell me, you who are willing to be under the law, do you not hear the law? {LSV}

They were so concerned about gaining righteousness and acceptance with God through keeping the Law, but had they actually listened to it?

A very salutary lesson for us all about Scripture! Do we listen? Do we hear? It is possible to read it and not hear it. It is possible to read it and not listen to it.

The NRSV renders this verse:

'Will you not listen to the Law?'

Sometimes a paraphrase can help to elucidate truth. This is how the message Bible does so:

'Tell me now, you who have become so enamoured with the Law: have you paid close attention to that Law?'

Then he takes them to the Old Testament. And he says: 'It is written.' V22, for it has been written... {LSV}

- **Listen to the Word of promise**
- **Look at the Word of promise**
- **Learn from the Word of promise**
- **Lean on the Word of promise**

And the inspired writer takes us back to the Old Testament and to the very first book of the Bible, Genesis and to Chapters 16, Verse 15, and 21, Verse 2.

So let us look at what Paul is saying here. Even if you read it a few times it's difficult to understand. But let us go through it and hear exactly what Paul is saying. Then we will seek to explain the mighty truth that is revealed here and how Scripture is handled by the great apostle Paul.

Remember he was a pharisee and he had been trained and was an expert in the Law. It took the grace of God to reveal to him as the Holy Spirit needs to reveal to us the meaning of Scripture.

We find reference to Abraham's bondwoman or slave Hagar who bore him a son called Ishmael. She was his concubine. She bore him a son.

God had promised Abraham a son but men and women are always in a hurry and Sarah and Abraham hatched a plan that Abraham should sleep with Hagar and have a child through her and that is what happened. Ishmael was born and he was not the son of promise.

Abraham's wife was called Sarah and his wife also bore him a son called Isaac. Isaac was the son of promise.

One woman was a slave and the other was free. The children of the bond woman are described as the children of slavery.

Paul says this is an allegory – there is a hidden or

125

deeper reality here, says Paul.

The two women represent two covenants and Hagar is of Mount Sinai and she represents those descendants of Abraham who observe the Law.

Her children are the children of slavery. She is from Mt Sinai which corresponds to what Paul describes as the then-present Jerusalem.

On the other hand we have Sarah who corresponds to the Jerusalem above. She is free, Paul says, and we are the children of the free woman.

And Paul quotes from the Prophet Isaiah which says that the children of the desolate women are more numerous than the children of the one who is married.

Notice again that Paul says in verse 27, 'for it has been written,' and he continues:

> "Rejoice, O barren, who is not bearing; break forth and cry, you who are not travailing, because many are the children of the desolate - more than of her having the husband."
> {LSV}

The text is from the book of Isaiah 54.1 {ESV}

Sing, O barren one, who did not bear; break forth into singing and cry aloud, you who have not been in labor! For the children of the desolate one will be more than the children of her who is married," says the LORD.

Paul describes the believers of the gentile nations as brothers of Isaac, the children of promise.

Children of promise
V28 now you Brothers, like Isaac are children of promise.

We are not children of the bondwoman but of the free woman.

Children of promise – children of faith, not works! Of the Spirit and not of the flesh.

We live not according to the old nature i.e. the flesh but rather the Spirit. Walk in the Spirit and you will not gratify the desires of the flesh.
Gal 5.16

...put off your old self, which belongs to your former manner of life and is corrupt through

deceitful desires, and to be renewed in the spirit of your minds, and to put on the new self, created after the likeness of God in true righteousness and holiness.
Eph 4.22-24 (ESV)

As we conclude chapter 4 could I suggest that for further reading in relation to the issues raised here, please consider taking the time to read Romans, Chapter 2, Verses 17-29.

God wants circumcision of the heart. Real circumcision is spiritual, not literal.
It isn't something you would hear many people preaching or perhaps writing about. But this chapter in Romans will help to elucidate the truth about circumcision.

Here are some suggested headings for you to consider for further study:

- **The mark of circumcision**
- **The mystery of circumcision**
- **The meaning of circumcision**
- **The means of circumcision**

Recently the verse I was considering when I awoke from a night's sleep and was having coffee with the Lord, was Romans, Chapter 3, Verse 23. I wrote in my journal entry for that morning as follows:

'This needs to be included in Galatians Chapter 4 and as we enter into chapter 5. This passage in Romans explains it perfectly. In fact to read from Romans chapter 2 Verse 17 right through to chapter 5 really nails it. Salvation is all of grace and is through faith in Christ.' To get the full impact of this read 2.17-4.21.

One thing I have learned when considering a verse of Scripture, and it is worth repeating here again, is that at some point in the mediation on the wonder of one verse, is to read the chapter behind it and the chapter containing it and the chapter following it, to get context and understand the text.

There is the great danger of taking a text out of its context and making it a pretext. How many heresies and misunderstandings and false doctrines and disputes have arisen because of this gross malpractice in mishandling the Word of God? We need to compare Scripture with Scripture.

The sceptic is a dab hand, of course, at pulling a verse out of thin air and telling us the Bible is full of contradictions, when it is not. The fool who does this is the contradiction.

You can be sure the Devil never quotes Scripture but always misquotes it.

Let us learn from the words of Paul to Timothy.

Study to shew thyself approved unto God, a workman that needeth not to be ashamed, rightly dividing the word of truth.

Timothy, Chapter 2, Verse 15 {KJV}

And in the NRSV:

Do your best to present yourself to God as one approved by him, a worker who has no need to be ashamed, rightly explaining the word of truth.

We need to rightly divide, we need to rightly explain, accurately and skilfully teaching the Word of Truth. {ANT}

And since most of us consider ourselves not to be teachers, nevertheless it behoves us all to rightly handle God's Word.

And if you think you are not a teacher, think again because we are all teachers.

You shall teach them to your children, talking of them when you are sitting in your house, and when you are walking by the way, and when you lie down, and when you rise.

Deuteronomy, Chapter 11, Verse 19 {ESV}

Our homes should be teaching homes where we teach the Word of God. And if we don't have children and even if we do, let us ask the Lord to lead us to people who we can lead to the Lord and we can teach those who are children in the faith.

Do you remember the man in Acts who was speaking in the synagogue in Jerusalem? His name was Apollos and he was a cultured man and he was an eloquent speaker and he knew the Hebrew Scriptures and he was passionate about the Lord Jesus; however, he needed some help in understanding more fully.

Dr. Luke tells us that:

He began to speak boldly in the synagogue, but when Priscilla and Aquila heard him, they took him aside and explained to him the way of God more accurately.

Acts, Chapter 18, Verse 26 {ESV}

The {LSV} rendering puts it thus:

And Aquilas and Pricilla having heard of him, took him [them] and more exactly set forth to him the way of God.

And so we move on now to the penultimate chapter of Galatians, Chapter 5.

CHAPTER 5

NO OTHER GROUND

Finding True Freedom In Christ V1-14

- **True freedom**
- **Truly found**
- **True Faith**

Fruit in the Spirit V15-26

No Other Ground
True Freedom in Christ V1-14.

V1. For freedom Christ has set us free; stand firm therefore, and do not submit again to a yoke of slavery.

V2. Look: I, Paul, say to you that if you accept circumcision, Christ will be of no advantage to you.

V3. I testify again to every man who accepts

circumcision that he is obligated to keep the whole law.

V4. You are severed from Christ, you who would be justified by the law; you have fallen away from grace.

V5. For through the Spirit, by faith, we ourselves eagerly wait for the hope of righteousness.

V6. For in Christ Jesus neither circumcision nor uncircumcision counts for anything, but only faith working through love.

V7. You were running well. Who hindered you from obeying the truth?

V8. This persuasion is not from him who calls you.

V9. A little leaven leavens the whole lump.

V10. I have confidence in the Lord that you will take no other view, and the one who is troubling you will bear the penalty, whoever he is.

V11. But if I, brothers, still preach circumcision,

why am I still being persecuted? In that case the offense of the cross has been removed.

V12. I wish those who unsettle you would emasculate themselves!

V13. For you were called to freedom, brothers. Only do not use your freedom as an opportunity for the flesh, but through love serve one another.

V14. For the whole law is fulfilled in one word: "You shall love your neighbor as yourself."

Galatians, Chapter 5.1-14 {ESV}

Finding True Freedom in Christ V1-14

Freedom in Christ

If not the chief word in Galatians, one of the chiefest is the word FREEDOM. Hence the title of this book as the first in the Alliteration for Inspiration series, 'Finding Freedom'.

V1. In the freedom, then, which Christ made you free - stand, and do not be held fast again by a yoke of servitude. {LSV}

You have found freedom in Christ! Then stand in this freedom.

The word 'stand' literally means to keep standing firm. The word is 'steko' and it means to stand, to stand firm. To declare I stand fast, it has the concept to persevere. The word is used 8 times in the NT.

Check them out for a very worthwhile study.

Mark 11.25

Romans 14.4

I Corinthians 16.13

(Galatians 5.1)

Philippians 1.27

Philippians 4.1

Thessalonians 3.8

Thessalonians 2.15

In Galatians 5.1, Paul is writing to exhort the Christians to not relinquish their freedom but to live in the freedom that has been made possible by the Saviour. It is a freedom to live in the Spirit, to live a life of agape love and not a life of licentiousness. To bear good fruit in the Spirit who indwells us.

Chapter 4 ends with the word 'free'. It is worth reiterating what we have considered in the previous chapter.

V31. ...we are not a maidservant's children, but the free [woman's]
{LSV}

God in His absolute sovereignty decided that through Abraham all the nations of the earth would be blessed (3.9). And the promises spoken were spoken to Abraham and to his Seed which is Christ. And the covenant was confirmed before by God to Christ (3.16). The Law came 430 years later and the law did not make the promise to Abraham void. God granted it through promise, not the Law, else it would not be a promise. Indeed it would make the promise void (3.17).

So why the Law? The Law was put in place until the Seed – Jesus Christ – would come to whom the promise had been made. And He would be the only man who ever lived on the earth to perfectly fulfil the Law of God and usher in the dispensation of grace. We are no longer under law but under grace. Free grace.

> For the Law was given through Moses, the grace and the truth came through Jesus Christ.
> John 1.17 {LSV}

...the Law became our tutor - to Christ, that we may be declared righteous by faith. And faith having come we are no longer under a tutor. Galatians 3.24,25 {LSV}

And when the fullness of time came, God sent forth His Son, come of a woman, come under the Law, that He may redeem those under the law, that we may receive the adoption of sons. Galatians 4.4,5 {LSV}

And then Paul used that allegory of Hagar and Sarah. The son of Hagar, Ishmael, was not in the line of the promise. The son of Sarah, Isaac, was the son of the promise. The genealogy of Jesus Christ would be through Isaac.

When we read the genealogy of the Man Jesus Christ we find that right at the beginning of the Gospel of Matthew:

The scroll of the birth of Jesus Christ, Son of David, Son of Abraham. Abraham begot Isaac and Isaac begot Jacob, and Jacob begot Judah and his brother,
Matthew 1.1,2 {LSV}

V11. For the grace of God has appeared, bringing salvation for all people, V12. training us to renounce ungodliness and worldly passions, and to live self-controlled, upright, and godly lives in the present age, V13. waiting for our blessed hope, the appearing of the glory of our great God and Saviour Jesus Christ, V14. who gave himself for us to redeem us from all lawlessness and to purify for himself a people for his own possession who are zealous for good works. V15. Declare these things; exhort and rebuke with all authority. Let no one disregard you.

Titus 2.11-15. {ESV}

Paul defends the freedom we have in Christ and emphasises this by stating its opposite in 5.1. The yoke of servitude. To demand adherence to circumcision voids a person from the free grace of Christ. In fact in Verse 4 he says this position is to fall away from grace. For we by the Spirit, by faith, wait for a hope of righteousness (V5).

And then he uses a very significant wording – for 'in Christ Jesus' neither circumcision avails anything, nor uncircumcision, but faith working through love (V6).

Found in Christ

I would like to ask the reader a question; and the question is this:

Are you found in Christ alone?

Are you in Christ?

The world is divided into two categories of People. Those who are in Christ and those who are outside of Christ. Are you in Christ or outside of Christ?

Let me remind you of what Paul said in the earlier part of Galatians and the explanation of that in chapter 4 about our freedom in Christ.

> There is neither Jew nor Greek, there is neither slave nor free, there is no male and female, for you are all one in Christ Jesus.
> Galatians 3.28 {ESV}

All one in Christ Jesus.

'In Christ.'

This is a little phrase that Paul uses a number of times in the Book of Galatians. It is also used throughout the New Testament. Let me show these to you just now from the Book of Galatians.

Believers in Christ

Paul describes the assemblies (the churches) of Judah as those who are 'in Christ'.

Chapter 1.22 {LSV}

The Church of Jesus Christ is made up of those who are 'in Christ.'

Believing in Christ

Again in chapter 2, Verse 16, the writer describes those in Christ as follows:

> Having known that a man is not declared righteous by works of law but through faith from Jesus Christ, we also believed in Christ Jesus that we might be declared righteous by faith from Christ and not by works of law, because no flesh will be declared righteous by works of law. {LSV}

And again in verse 17, the writer talks about being found righteous in Christ.

Paul says we sought justification in Christ but if we are seeking to add something more, i.e. seeking, by ourselves, to perform some duty of the law, then that would mean there was something inadequate in our justification in Christ, so if we are falling back on our adherence to the Law, then Christ is void and we are in a greater predicament than when we started out. We are condemned under the Law of God.

Permit me to draw on a verse from Hebrews (11.7) to illustrate the point from the Old Testament writings. Here is the Divine Commentary on Noah.

> By faith Noah, having been divinely warned concerning the things not yet seen, having feared, prepared an ark to the salvation of his house, through which he condemned the world, and he became heir of the righteousness according to faith.
>
> Hebrews 11.7 {LSV}

We read in Genesis 7.1. And YHWH said to Noah, come you and all your house into the Ark. And in V16, we are told that when they were all come into the Ark as God had commanded him, And 'YHWH closes it for him. That is, God shut the door! They were safe inside the Ark.'

We are safe in Christ. It would have been sheer madness to seek to open a door that God had shut and paddle your own little ark in the flood of God's judgment against sin. Being in the Ark was all that mattered. Trusting God alone for salvation. So it is with us. We are in Christ; why would we seek any alternative outside of Him, He who bore the wrath of God for us?

The point is, being in Christ means we are justified by the perfect redemptive work of Christ, not by works. Herein is our freedom. Our Freedom to live the life of love in Christ.

Blessings in Christ

Then we read in the third chapter that the blessing of Abraham would come to the nations in Christ.

Chapter 3. 14. {LSV}

In the verse preceding V14 Paul refers to Christ redeeming us from the curse of the Law, having become a curse for us.

Paul juxtaposes the cursing and the blessing. His was the curse, ours is the blessing.

We are reminded of the great prophecy of the Prophet Isaiah:

> V5. And He is pierced for our transgressions, bruised for our iniquities. II The discipline of our peace [is] on Him, and by His scourging we are healed. V6. All of us, like sheep, have wandered. II Man has turned to his own way, II and YHWH

has laid on Him the punishment of us all.
Isaiah, Chapter 53, 5-6 {LSV}

Brothers in Christ

For you are all sons of God through faith in Christ Jesus.

Chapter 3.26 {LSV}

We are brothers and sisters in Christ.

Bound [together] in Christ

For you are all one in Christ Jesus.

Chapter 3.28 {LSV}

Beauty in Christ

For in Christ neither circumcision avails anything, nor uncircumcision, but faith working through love.

Chapter 5.6 {LSV}

Living the life of love and Paul goes on to speak of the fruit of the Spirit. The beauty of Christ seen in His people.

Born in Christ

We are a new creation in Christ.

Chapter 6.15 {LSV}

Born again – brand new! New creation!

I pray that you are found in Christ alone!

Oh turn to Jesus – If you are not found in Christ alone then you are lost outside of Christ alone, without a Saviour! Oh turn to Him and find the freedom that your soul desires and that you were made for. Have done with the folly of sin and this fallen world's false promises of freedom in permissiveness and anything goes – it's the road of bondage and slavery and damnation.

Be sure you are in Christ and live in the freedom of Christ.

There is freedom in Christ alone.

Let us guard freedom in Christ and see to it that we do not fall away.

Enjoy your full freedom in Christ and no free falling into pride, complacency, backsliding and sin; to bondage by returning to the beggarly elements of the world.

We left the swine trough and the swill of the world so why on earth go back to it again?

The world has nothing to offer us.

Why would we allow ourselves to be burdened again by a yoke of slavery?

We've got to face facts. It is possible to go back. Solomon put it this way:

As a dog returns to its vomit,
so fools repeat their folly.
Do you see a man wise in his own eyes?
There is more hope for a fool than for him.
Proverbs, Ch 26, 11,12 {NIV}

I saw this inspirational quote recently and it sums it up very eloquently and succinctly.

Don't go back to
Something God
Has already
Rescued you
From.

The Galatians were running so well in the freedom they found in Christ, who has hindered you so as not to obey the truth? (V7) The NLT helps us to grasp what Paul says next.

It certainly isn't God, for He is the one who called you to freedom.
Galatians 5.8 {NLT}

Have we been hindered in any way from following our Lord and Saviour Jesus Christ?

When we leave the Word of God to the side and don't make the time to read it and hear what God is saying to us every day we are in danger of becoming fools because we start to rely on our own wisdom and that is the slippery slope to returning to the beggarly elements of the world.

It's what the NIV (Galatians 4.9) describes as turning back to the weak and miserable principles of the world.

We live in freedom under biblical principles, not worldly principles which would bring us into servitude again. I.e., bondage!

The way of faith is the way of freedom!

Faith in Christ

Paul really lays it on the line! If you insist on this notion of circumcision as being the way of salvation then you have lost it literally and you have lost Christ. You are not in freedom, you are in bondage!

Way back in Deuteronomy Chapter 30 – read it for yourself – it's the circumcision of the heart that we need.

> And the LORD your God will circumcise your heart and the heart of your offspring, so that you will love the LORD your God with all your

heart and with all your soul, that you may live.
Deuteronomy, Chapter 30, Verse 6 {ESV}

He is faithful. We must be faithful to Him.
We need to be faithful to him and not replace Him
with anything or anyone! Not rules and regulations
which are man-made and designed to glorify self
and not the Lord who bought us with His own blood.

For no one can lay a foundation other than that
which is laid, which is Jesus Christ.
1 Corinthians, Chapter 3, Verse 11 {ESV}

To do otherwise is to build upon the sand – utter
folly!
It is folly, utter folly to be outside of Christ. It is
utter folly also to allow ourselves to be hindered in
our relationship with Christ. They had allowed false
teachers to influence them and they took their
eyes off Jesus and began to look at themselves and
believe in what they could do and what they could
achieve.
In the secular world the person is king of the castle.
It's all about the self and self-actualisation. The
Gospel turns this on its head and proclaims Jesus as
King over all.

Circumcise the Lord God in your hearts.

> *King of my life I crown three now,*
> *Thine shall the glory be,*
> *Lest I forget thy thorned crowned brow,*
> *Lead me to calvary.*

V8. such misguided teaching in relation to law keeping to earn salvation did not come from Him who is calling you.

V9. Then Paul mentions leaven and says that a little leaven leavens the whole lump.

Paul was in effect using a proverb that would have been familiar to the Galatian assemblies. Yeast spreads into the entire batch of dough. Thus false teaching once it gets a foothold will spread and it will infect everything and everyone. The false teaching needs to be rejected and expelled from the assemblies.

V10. Paul is confident that they will see the truth and agree with him.

V11. Paul makes it clear that he did not preach

circumcision as some had suggested. Their reasoning for this may have been that Paul, on taking Timothy with him on his second missionary journey, his first step was to have Timothy circumcised (Acts 16.3). And this was the very journey in which he first visited Galatia. He had refused to let Titus be circumcised (Galatians 2.3-5). And why? In short, in Galatia Paul was up against false teaching of salvation by works and the activities of false teachers. The Jews that Paul was dealing with in Acts 16 were not even Christians and having Timothy circumcised was for pragmatic reasons.

The point Paul is making here in V11 is that if he was the exponent of salvation by works of the law, in this instance, circumcision, then why was he being persecuted by the Jews? The cross is described as a stumbling block.

The natural man does not want the preaching of the cross – the natural man wants to do it his own way, when there is only one way of salvation – faith in Christ alone and His finished cross work alone! To preach circumcision is to remove the stumbling-block of the cross.

Since the Jews ask a sign, and Greeks seek wisdom, also we preach Christ crucified, to Jews, indeed, a stumbling-block, and to Greeks foolishness, and to

those called - both Jews and Greeks - Christ the power of God, and the wisdom of God, Because the foolishness of God is wiser than men, and the weakness of God is stronger than men;
1 Corinthians 1.22-25 {LSV}

V12. In a moment of exasperation perhaps, Paul says he wishes that those who are troubling them by teaching that circumcision is necessary for salvation would even go all the way and castrate themselves.

There is a place for righteous anger.

V13. You were called to freedom! However, this is not an opportunity to do what we like – it means that we through love serve and seek the best for one another. We are not to give in to the sinful nature, worldliness and selfishness.

And here is another mighty statement.

V14. All the Law is fulfilled in one word - in this: you will love your neighbour as yourself.
{LSV}

And then in V15, Paul says that we are not to bite and devour one another in bickering and strife.

Don't be consumed in this way. Rather, be consumed with love.

Fruitfulness in the Spirit

V15. But if you bite and devour one another, watch out that you are not consumed by one another.

V16. But I say, walk by the Spirit, and you will not gratify the desires of the flesh.

V17. For the desires of the flesh are against the Spirit, and the desires of the Spirit are against the flesh, for these are opposed to each other, to keep you from doing the things you want to do.

V18. But if you are led by the Spirit, you are not under the law.

V19. Now the works of the flesh are evident: sexual immorality, impurity, sensuality,

V20. Idolatry, sorcery, enmity, strife, jealousy, fits of anger, rivalries, dissensions, divisions,

V21. envy, drunkenness, orgies, and things like

these. I warn you, as I warned you before, that those who do such things will not inherit the kingdom of God.

We have been called to freedom! Freedom that enables us to live the way God intended us to live and be the people we were meant to be. To live a life of love. To walk in the Spirit. And if we walk in the Spirit we will not gratify the sinful desires.

And Paul lists the works of the flesh, some fifteen of these, and then he adds 'and things like these. I warn you, as I warned you before, that those who do such things will not inherit the kingdom of God.'

What we do reveals our heart and who we really are and who we serve. What we do will reveal if we are walking in the freedom of the redemption which Christ has purchased for us; or if we are alienated from God and in bondage to sin.

We who are redeemed will have the desire to live in the freedom of a holy life that God intended us to live. Faultless? Who among us is faultless? But we follow the faultless One, the sinless One. Our Lord Jesus Christ. Jesus said to the Pharisees of His day who refused to believe in Him and argued that they were the children of Abraham, when Jesus told them straight they were the children of their father the Devil for he was a liar from the beginning:

> Can any of you prove me guilty of sin? If I am
> telling the truth, why don't you believe me?
> John 8.46. {NLT}

V22. But the fruit of the Spirit is love, joy, peace,
patience, kindness, goodness, faithfulness,

V23. gentleness, self-control; against such things
there is no law.

The Lord wants us to bear fruit, good fruit and here
we have the nine fruits of the Spirit.
We are not under law but under grace. We live in
the grace of God and produce the fruit of the Spirit.

Paul reminds us that those who belong to Christ
have crucified the flesh with its passions and
desires. We have died to self and in this way we are
enabled by the Spirit of the Holy Spirit to produce
fruit.

> I Am the Vine, you the branches; he who is
> remaining in Me, and I in him, this one bears
> much fruit, because apart from Me you are not

able to do anything.
John 15.5 {LSV}

You did not choose Me, but I choose you, and appointed you, that you might go away, and might bear fruit and your fruit might remain, that whatever you ask of the Father in My Name, He might give you.
John 15.16. {LSV}

And then Jesus promised us the Holy Spirit, the third Person of the Godhead. The One of whom Paul speaks here in the context of the fruit of the Spirit.

And when the Comforter may come, whom I will send to you from the Father - the Spirit of Truth, who comes forth from the Father, He will testify of Me; and you also testify, because you are with Me from the beginning.
John 15.26,27 {LSV}

Let us see to it that we walk in the Spirit (V16) and produce the Fruit of the Spirit. And let us do some reflection and self-introspection and ask ourselves some pertinent questions; and where we are failing let us ask the Holy Spirit to come to our aid and transform us into the likeness of Jesus upon whom, in His humanity, at His baptism the Holy Spirit, was seen descending as a dove and coming on Him. Indeed in the book of Isaiah, we have the prophecy of the Suffering Servant.

> Behold, My Servant, I take hold on Him, My Chosen One - my soul has accepted, I have put my Spirit on Him...
> Isaiah 42.1 {LSV}

- **Love**

Do I live a life of love and show love to all?

- **Joy**

Do I express joy and experience joy in my heart?

- **Peace**

Do I seek to live a life of peace and seek peace and pursue it?

- **Patience**

Do I exhibit patience in my life and know patience?

- **Kindness**

Do I show kindness and seek to be kind in all my ways?

- **Goodness**

Do I know goodness and show goodness in all my interactions?

- **Faithfulness**

Do I seek to be faithful to the Lord in all things?

- **Gentleness**

Do I exhibit gentleness and be known as gentle?

- **Self-control**

Do I know self-control and have self-control?

V24. And those who belong to Christ Jesus have crucified the flesh with its passions and desires.

V25. If we live by the Spirit, let us also keep in step with the Spirit.

We are those who belong to Christ Jesus and we are His followers. We identify with Him in His death, burial and resurrection. This means that we deny ourselves and have taken up the cross to follow Him.

And He said to all, if anyone wills to come after Me, let him disown himself, and take up his

cross daily, and follow Me;
Luke 9.23 {LSV}

Notice what Jesus says, to be His followers we must deny or as the LSV renders it; we must 'disown' ourselves.

This turns popular culture on its head. Today it's all about me. Jesus says we must disown ourselves and follow Him and take up the cross daily. And what is this cross? It is the cross of self-denial. To truly follow Christ I must deny myself. This is the way to find the true self and true freedom to be what God intended us to be.

V26. Let us not become conceited, provoking one another, envying one another.

To continue to live in the freedom that Christ has bought for us we need to follow Him closely, listen for His voice and hear and heed Him and keep ourselves clean!
Jesus told his disciples:

> Already you are clean because of the word that I have spoken to you
> Ephesians 5:25-26 {NIV}

Paul said:

> Husbands, love your wives, just as Christ loved the church and gave himself up for her to make her holy, cleansing her by the washing with water through the word, and to present her to Himself as a radiant church, without stain or wrinkle or any other blemish, but holy and blameless.
> Ephesians 5.25,26 {NIV}

This was brought home to me recently when I took out some of my fountain pens which hadn't been used for some time. I had to steep the nibs in water. It was unbelievable the amount of blackness that came out in the container, indeed it took many hours to clean before they could be used and be effective again. You get the point, pardon the pun, the amount of contamination we pick up in the world needs to be dealt with and the way to do this is to soak in the word of God. Immersed in the word will keep us clean and usable in the Master's service. We now come to the final chapter of the book of Galatians, Chapter 6.

Galatians Chapter 6
No Other Greatness

That's the Spirit

The Spirit of Gentleness
The Spirit of Humbleness
The Spirit of Watchfulness
The Spirit of Supportiveness
The Spirit of Christlikeness
The Spirit of Lowliness
The Spirit of Reflectiveness
The Spirit of Joyfulness
The Spirit of Singleness
The Spirit of Teachableness
The Spirit of Generousness
The Spirit of Fruitfulness
The Spirit of Determinedness
The Spirit of Goodness
The Spirit of Boastfulness
The Spirit of Graciousness.

CHAPTER 6

NO OTHER GREATNESS

V1. Brothers, if anyone is caught in any transgression, you who are spiritual should restore him in a spirit of gentleness. Keep watch on yourself, lest you too be tempted.

V2. Bear one another's burdens, and so fulfil the law of Christ.

V3. For if anyone thinks he is something, when he is nothing, he deceives himself.

V4. But let each one test his own work, and then his reason to boast will be in himself alone and not in his neighbor.

V5. For each will have to bear his own load.

V6. Let the one who is taught the word share all good things with the one who teaches.

V7. Do not be deceived: God is not mocked, for whatever one sows, that will he also reap.

V8. For the one who sows to his own flesh will from the flesh reap corruption, but the one who sows to the Spirit will from the Spirit reap eternal life.

V9. And let us not grow weary of doing good, for in due season we will reap, if we do not give up.

V10. So then, as we have opportunity, let us do good to everyone, and especially to those who are of the household of faith.

V11. See with what large letters I am writing to you with my own hand.

V12. It is those who want to make a good showing in the flesh who would force you to be circumcised, and only in order that they may not be persecuted for the cross of Christ.

V13. For even those who are circumcised do not themselves keep the law, but they desire to have you circumcised that they may boast in your flesh.

V14. But far be it from me to boast except in the cross of our Lord Jesus Christ, by which the world has been crucified to me, and I to the world.

V15. For neither circumcision counts for anything, nor uncircumcision, but a new creation.

V16. And as for all who walk by this rule, peace and mercy be upon them, and upon the Israel of God.

V17. From now on let no one cause me trouble, for I bear on my body the marks of Jesus.

V18. The grace of our Lord Jesus Christ be with your spirit, brothers. Amen.

That's The Spirit

Do we have the right Spirit? We need to cultivate the right Spirit. We as believers have the Holy Spirit. Paul described the fruit of the Spirit for us in Chapter 5:

> But the fruit of the Spirit is love, joy, peace, patience, kindness, goodness, faithfulness, gentleness, self-control; against such things there is no law.
> Galatians 5.22-23 {ESV}

The Spirit of Gentleness

A gentle spirit is a lovely attribute to have. It comes from the wisdom of God.

God is gentle

But the wisdom from above is first pure, then peaceable, gentle, open to reason, full of mercy and good fruits, impartial and sincere. And a harvest of righteousness is sown in peace by those who make peace.

James 3.17,18 {ESV}

The Psalmist said:

Your gentleness has made me great.
Psalm 18.35 {ESV}

Jesus is gentle

Come to me, all who labor and are heavy laden, and I will give you rest. Take my yoke upon you, and learn from me, for I am gentle and lowly in heart, and you will find rest for your souls.

Matthew 11.28,29 {ESV}

The Holy Spirit is Gentle

And John bore witness: "I saw the Spirit descend

from heaven like a dove, and it remained on him.
John 1.32 {ESV}

And we are to be gentle
Let your reasonableness be known to everyone.
The Lord is at hand;
Philippians 4.5. {ESV} Or *gentleness*

Let us sow good seeds of gentleness to please the
Spirit and let us not give up.
Sometimes people fall. People fail. People are
caught in temptation. Scripture reminds us:

V1. Brothers, if anyone is caught in any
transgression, you who are spiritual should restore
him in a spirit of gentleness.

What do we do when someone falls?
Have you heard about so-and-so? It's scandalous
really. They are an embarrassment! The church
should put them out!
We should not leave the wounded on the
battlefield to die alone. How many casualties are
there out there who have not been restored
because none of us went?
The Amplified translation renders the passage in
this way:

Brothers, if anyone is caught in any sin, you who are spiritual [that is, you who are responsive to the guidance of the Spirit] are to restore such a person in a spirit of gentleness [not with a sense of superiority or self-righteousness]

God's word says to restore them!

Surely the church should be a hospital for the casualties of war!

The word 'restore' as used here means to strengthen, to perfect, to complete, to make one what they ought to be! WOW – now that's awesome – we need to be involved in the ministry of restoration. By correction the person can be brought back to the right way.

We must go out of our way for those who have gone the wrong way or who have fallen by the way and seek to restore them!

If you are the one who has failed, and who of us has not failed in some way, may this word of encouragement be used to bring you back and I pray that God will send that person you need just now to bring you back and to restore you to the Lord again.

He restores my life

Psalm 23.4 {NRSV}

My verse for today was this verse. I have just been made redundant having worked for the same organisation for 21 years, the anniversary of which was 18th October 1999 and in the Covid-19 year.

But He restores my life and leads me in the paths of life for Name sake.
He has promised not only complete restoration but also clear direction. Amen!
Oh, my dear friend, listen! Listen to the Lord and listen to what He is to us. Say the following – the me is you!

He returns me (from the scrapheap of failure to the highway of faith).
He returns me!
He restores me!
He rebuilds me!
He remakes me!
He recommissions me!
He refreshes me!
He rests me!
He resends me!
He redirects me!
He recruits me!
He rescues me!

He revives me!
He redeems me!

The Spirit of Humbleness

Keep watch on yourself, lest you too be tempted.
keeping a watchful eye on yourself, so that you are
not tempted as well.
{AMP}

> If you think you are standing strong, be careful
> not to fall.
> 1 Corinthians, Chapter 10, Verse 12 {NLT}

Again, let me remind us of something very
important. The context of the verse.
And to get the context you need to read what
comes before and what comes after.
The context of this verse is Paul's deep care, genuine
concern and passion for the assemblies of Galatia.
Paul was so concerned about the false teaching that
he wrote this letter. He doesn't mince his words but
they come from a heart of love. We have a collective
responsibility for each other.
In seeking to help others who have gone astray
from the freedom that is in Christ, we need to be
mindful of our own vulnerability. Paul's letter was

firm but he was not just having a go at people, nor was he seeking to hammer them into submission, rather he was seeking with great humility to get them back on track and to live in the true freedom of Jesus Christ.

Recently I happened to be in a conversation when the matter of 'what does the Bible mean?' was raised. Someone had downloaded a long list of Bible verses off the internet compiled by some person with nothing better to do than to pull out a multiplicity of verses from their context and then with great glee declare, 'Here is a verse from the Bible, what does it mean? Sure it can mean anything and it contradicts itself.' It caused me to say:

Wonderful things in the Bible. I see some were put there by you and by me.

I remember an old preacher with an exceptional gift of expository preaching who said, 'If you are going to take a verse and quote it, you need to read the entire chapter and the chapter before it and the chapter in front of it. Then you will get the sense of the verse.'

Indeed you may need to read the whole book to get the sense of the theme and the verse. Yes, one verse.

Oh and by the way, don't forget to interpret the

obscure in the light of the plain. We will leave the details of hermeneutics for another time but it does rile me somewhat when people mishandle the Word of God; when professing themselves to be wise they become fools.

Enough of my butterfly brain wanderings, at least for the moment.

The Spirit of Watchfulness

In this instance when we read the quotation, 'If you think you are standing strong, be careful not to fall,' we could surmise, oh, that's about pride. Pride comes before a fall. And in James it does refer to pride, but here it's about idolatry.

In Romans 15.4 Paul speaks about this idolatry and he takes the reader back to the Old Testament and the wilderness wanderings of the children of Israel. He talks about their indulgences in sinful practices precipitated by idolatry. And we are told the things that were written aforetime were written for our learning – for our instruction upon whom the end of the ages have come {V11}.

Therefore! (when we see a therefore you need to ask, what is it therefore?)

Therefore let anyone that thinks that he stands take heed lest he fall. V12. {ESV}

The Spirit of Supportiveness
V2. Bear one another's burdens. The AMP says carry them – carry their burdens.

Have we the Spirit of Supportiveness?

The Spirit of Christlikeness
V2b. and so fulfil the law of Christ. And what is this law of Christ?

To put it another way; how does carrying one another's burdens fulfil the law of Christ?
In Galatians, Chapter 5, Verse 14, Paul says:
For the entire law is fulfilled in keeping this one command: Love your neighbor as yourself.
Thus the law of Christ is the Law of Love. We are to show love! We are like the Lord Jesus when we show love to others.
And like Jesus we are to exhibit:

The Spirit of Lowliness
V3. let us not think we are something when we are nothing. I am nothing without my Lord and Master. We are only deceiving ourselves if we think we are something.

V27. But God chose the foolish things of the world to shame the wise; God chose the weak things of the world to shame the strong.

V.28 God chose the lowly things of this world and the despised things—and the things that are not— to nullify the things that are,

V29. so that no one may boast before him...
1 Corinthians, Chapter 1, Verses 27-29 {NIV}

The King James version says He chose the things that are nothing! We are nothing!
I'm just a nobody telling everybody about somebody who saved my soul. And His Name is Jesus.

The Spirit of Reflectiveness
V4. But each one must carefully scrutinize his/her own work - examining his/her actions, attitudes and behaviours.

Do we take time to reflect? We need time for reflective practice. We need time to scrutinise what we do.
Are my actions in keeping with the law of Christ?
Are my attitudes in keeping with the law of Christ?
Are my behaviours in keeping with the law of Christ?
These are important and penetrating questions

which we need to ask if we are to learn and grow spiritually. We need to examine our hearts and minds and spirits!

The Spirit of Joyfulness

I write this when, having worked for the same mental health charity for 21 years, on 18th October 2020 they inform me that I am being made redundant in the Covid year and it was somewhat of a cull because of restructuring in the face of budgetary constraints. Some weeks prior to this I wrote in my daily journal:

> *"No one is unemployed in the service of Jesus. No one is made redundant. No one is laid off. No one is retired! God is the Greatest Employer. And God has work for each of us to do. And when we walk in the will of God, obeying the word of God, doing the work of God we get a joy and a satisfaction that nothing else can give."*

The Spirit of Singleness

V4-5. Make a careful exploration of who you are and the work you have been given, and then sink yourself into that. Don't be impressed with yourself. Don't compare yourself with others. Each of you must take responsibility for doing the creative best you can with your own life. {MSG}

With singleness of heart serve the Lord.

The Spirit of Teachableness
V6. Let the one who is taught the word...

Let us be teachable and learn from the word and from those who have the gift of teaching.

The Spirit of Generousness
V6. And share all good things with the one who teaches.

The Spirit of Fruitfulness
V7,8. Don't be misled: No one makes a fool of God. What a person plants, he will harvest. The person who plants selfishness, ignoring the needs of others—ignoring God!—harvests a crop of weeds. All he'll have to show for his life is weeds! But the one who plants in response to God, letting God's Spirit do the growth work in Him, harvests a crop of real life, eternal life. {MSG}

The big question is, what are we sowing?

Let us plant in response to God. Let us be led by the Holy Spirit to be what we were meant to be and live for God and glorify Him in everything. Sowing with eternity in mind and not getting tangled up in the world's webs of nothingness and futility.

We can live in freedom — freedom to serve the Lord!

The Spirit of Determinedness

V9 and let us not grow weary….

Mary was a missionary returning home on furlough. When she got off the train a large crowd of people were standing on the platform cheering and clapping. Mary could not believe it, but then she realised that there was a famous celebrity standing behind her. Somewhat downcast, Mary hurried on her way. Her thoughts couldn't help but think about the sacrifices she had made for the sake of the Kingdom of God labouring away unseen and unnoticed. These were not bitter thoughts but she did feel somewhat forgotten and not appreciated. Then the Lord spoke to her, "Mary, you're not home yet."

Dear reader, you are not home yet.

Let us not become weary in doing good, for at the proper time we will reap a harvest if we do not give up.
Galatians 6.9 {NIV}

Keep going, my friend – you're not home yet. God still has a work for you to do. Don't worry about your age or how you are going to get by. Walk in the will of God. He will provide.

The Spirit of Goodness
V10. So then as we have opportunity, let us do good to everyone, especially those of the household of faith. {ESV}

That is a tough one unless we are walking in the Spirit.
I want revenge – They hurt me! They rejected me! They insulted me!
And how am I to treat them? I am to do good to everyone and that includes them. And why? Because God says so. End of!
The Father is so merciful with me and so good to me. I must reflect my Father's character and be merciful and show goodness too. Amen!

V11-18 These verses are really the postscript and

Paul has dictated his letter to his secretary or to use the old word, amanuensis. But he writes the conclusion in his own hand.

V11. See what large letters I make when I am writing in my own hand. Did he find it difficult to write? Was it eyesight? Whatever the case Paul writes in his own hand and its big letters.

He then proceeds to mention in closing his opponents who are enemies of the gospel and the cross of Christ. They are focused on the law and circumcision when, to use the words of Deuteronomy – we need the circumcision of the heart.

The Spirit of Boastfulness

Paul says in V14: May I never boast of anything except the cross of our Lord Jesus Christ, by which the world has been crucified to me, and I to the world. {NRSV} And V15: For neither circumcision nor uncircumcision is anything; but a new creation is everything!

And then we have in V16-18 a double blessing.

V16 is a formal traditional Jewish blessing in the form of a benediction. It's conditional as it is for those who follow this biblical teaching. It has been noted that it is the counterpart to the curse in 1.8. Where those who would dare to proclaim another gospel which is not a gospel but rather a distortion and to proclaim such as the circumcision were arguing for then let them be accursed!

V17. and no more trouble – Paul had the scars to prove his total devotion to the Lord Jesus Christ.

The Spirit of Graciousness
V18. the concluding benediction.

May the grace of our Lord Jesus be with your spirit, brothers and sisters. Amen.

How important it is that we reflect on Biblical Wisdom.
The Bible is the inspired Word of God. I have sought to provide you with alliteration for inspiration. May the Lord bless you as you spend time in His Word.

In Galatians we have considered:

Chapter 1 No Other Gospel

Let us proclaim the one true Gospel of God in word and deed.

Chapter 2 No Other Grace

The Gospel is a Gospel of Grace, not of works. We work for Christ, not to earn our salvation but rather our works are the outworking of His grace that has saved us.

Chapter 3 No Other Golgotha

Jesus accomplished His redeeming work on the cross. He redeemed us and freed us and we rely on His cross work for our salvation.

Chapter 4 No Other Guardian

The law showed us how sinful we are. The work of Christ takes away our sins and makes us righteous before God. the Law showed us how far short we had fallen. The work of Christ brings us near to God. Sons, Daughters and Heirs.

Chapter 5 No Other Ground

We stand on redemption ground. We stand in the freedom that Christ has won for us.

Chapter 6 No Other Greatness

May I never boast except in the cross of our Lord Jesus Christ, through which the world has been crucified to me, and I to the world.

Galatians 6.14.

Conclusion

The Angel Gabriel was sent by God from heaven to the town of Nazareth in Galilee to speak to a young virgin girl called Mary. Gabriel referred to Jesus' deity and royalty.

> He will be great and will be called the Son of the Most High. And the Lord God will give to him the throne of his father David, and He will reign over the house of Jacob forever and of His kingdom there will be no end.
>
> Luke 1.32, 33 {ESV}

Ours is a great Saviour. His the great Sacrifice. Ours is a great Salvation.

He is our Great God and our Great King.

Such a Great Saviour who procured such great salvation for us calls us to freedom.

We are free to do for Him, in Him and through Him,

great works of service.

Love so amazing, so divine demands my soul my life my all.

Find your true freedom in Christ and live in that freedom in the power of the Cross.

Amen and Amen.

PS: see you {DV} in the next book in the Alliteration for Inspiration series.

ABOUT THE AUTHOR

Graham began writing this book in January 2020 whilst working as a mental health advocacy service manager. He was made redundant in November after 21 years of service during the COVID-19 pandemic. A bit of a shock to the system. However, this gave him the added impetus to work on the book and the time needed to complete it.

He is a reader of the Scriptures over several decades and served in pastoral ministry for 15 years prior to working in the mental health field.

This is the author's first book to be published and others in the *Alliteration for Inspiration Series* are currently in the pipeline including *Finding True Love in 1 John* and *Finding True Hope in 1 Peter*.

Printed in Great Britain
by Amazon